The Cultural Sales Leader

The Cultural Sales Leader

Sustaining People, Attaining Results

Richard Cogswell

BEP

BUSINESS EXPERT PRESS

Leader in applied, concise business books

First published in 2024 by
Business Expert Press, LLC
222 East 46th Street, New York, NY 10017
www.businessexpertpress.com

ISBN-13: 978-1-63742-600-5 (paperback)
ISBN-13: 978-1-63742-601-2 (e-book)

Business Expert Press Selling and Sales Force Management Collection

First edition: 2024

10 9 8 7 6 5 4 3 2 1

*My heartfelt thanks to my family, and to
Adna, Anant, Jim, Frankie, Rhys, Peter, Ifor, Dyfan, and all at B&L.
You have all backed, inspired, and supported me on my journey.
You continue to do so.
I could not have done this without you.*

Description

Behaviors Form Culture, Leading to Results

The Cultural Sales Leader is about sales leadership, creating a performance culture, and followership. It is about creating a vision and then building an organization and approach which will make that vision a reality. It's about building a people-first culture that is bound to the mission you have set out and it is about thinking beyond the present to where you want to be as an organization in three to five years' time.

This book is for anyone interested in business, sales, sales leadership, or organizational culture building—no matter the level of experience or seniority. It contains the templates and approaches to help you shape the way you identify, create, analyze, and execute on your people-first strategy, while bringing the entire organization along with you to attain sustainable, transformational results.

The author outlines a layering process to becoming an expert in your business and identifying the key growth areas to allow you to get beyond the pure focus of your current financial year. It is about how you build a growth engine. The pathway to achieving this most effectively is through your people and culture. **Get the people element right and the results will come.**

Keywords

workplace culture; business culture; business strategy; corporate culture; company culture; corporate values; employee culture; organizational culture; organizational values; organizational change; organizational behavior; workplace environment; workplace relationships; workplace productivity; workplace communication; coaching; teamwork; leadership style; business; motivational; money; management leadership; entrepreneurship; emotional intelligence; sales; sales management; sales leadership; culture building; people-first leadership; sustainable long-term results; leadership; management; self-development; productivity; personal growth; team building; effective communication; inspiring; innovation; motivational; mindset; influence; success; sales; selling

Contents

Foreword

The Mission and Thanks

We live and work in fast paced times and, as commercial leaders, we are asked to achieve many things in short order. This book outlines a layering process to becoming an expert in your business and identifying the key growth areas to allow you to get beyond the pure focus in your current financial year. It is also about how you build a growth engine. The pathway to achieving this most effectively is through your people and culture. Get the people element right and the results will come.

The Goal

Sales is a team sport, but setting of the agenda in terms of where you will focus and how you will win in your market, rests on your shoulders as the profit and loss (P&L) owner of your commercial function. Within this, you must be clear on what the goal is, and what you will need to be able to win. You also have to manage yourself, your business, your team, your focuses, and your plan successfully. That's a lot.

My goal has been to write an accessible, practical, step-by-step guide, to help all sales leaders, no matter where they are in their career, to make a significant and lasting impact in their roles from day one. I have been most interested in building ambitious growth-minded teams that deliver sustained results. Behaviors and culture play a critical role in achieving these objectives.

The templates and approaches I outline have all helped me to build successful outperforming teams in a number of businesses at different stages of maturity, across several geographies and industries. To my mind, the secret of enabling and sustaining repeatable, transformational results is through focusing on your people across the organization first. It is about looking at your business through the lens of its greatest resource, your colleagues.

While seemingly obvious, for many reasons, this is not necessarily the primary focus you will observe at many organizations. Quite often, the organizational lens is solely focused on the numbers: the pipeline, the targets, the net revenue and inevitably, as a result, this month, this quarter, and this financial year in isolation. As a result, many opportunities can be left on the table and underexploited. I will show you how to build followership and a performance culture that will allow you to focus on what's important beyond your current financial year.

You will always face challenges in sales, but if you get the people element right, including harnessing their talents and passion focused toward one goal, the results will follow.

The figure and mantra shown in Figure F.1 provide the clearest encapsulation of what we will seek to set in motion over the coming chapters. It is also the clearest philosophy of what I consider sales leadership to be. If you focus on these components you will create a culture that is bound to the mission and therefore the results you wish to attain.

Whether newly hired or promoted, or for those with experience already gained on the journey, I aim to show a methodology focused on how we might best lay down the foundations for exponential and sustained growth through the sales leadership function and critically through the catalyst of culture.

In terms of my journey, I have worked in sales my entire professional life and have held most sales and sales leadership roles over the course of my career. My first sales leadership role came from an internal promotion and from there, I went on to a number of sales management, sales directorship, commercial leader, general manager, and VP roles, all requiring the ability to set focus and strategy while building or shaping a team to attain the goals set for the business. I have worked across multiple industries and geographies, for global multinational companies as well as for startups.

As someone who used to identify as an introvert, I have been thoroughly blessed to have met and worked with some of the most amazing people one would ever hope to meet. What marks out the greatest leaders I have learnt from in my opinion, is curiosity and generosity—generosity of time, support, and mentorship; a genuine concern and care for people and especially for their teams. These are the people who have shaped who I am today and helped me achieve things I couldn't possibly have imagined being attainable at the beginning of my journey. It is people like this that you should also seek out and who will more than likely become dear friends and positive, permanent fixtures in life.

You could say that my philosophy of sales is as a result entirely "people first." People have developed me in my journey and as a result, I aim as much as I can to help others on theirs, to the best of my ability. I see sales as being in the service of others and sales leadership being about helping others to be the best they can be, in the attainment of their own professional and personal goals. Humility, a love of people, curiosity, ambition, laser focus, and a drive to learn, are all qualities I would describe as being components of the people-first leader.

Having a philosophy of sales is a great place to begin to define your approach. If you do not have a guiding principle on what sales is to you, start by interrogating your personal values and build from there. Values are your core statements in terms of what is important to you and formulate a linkage between who you are as a person and how you show up to your profession. This linkage is important, and the most authentic leaders offer something of themselves in all that they do, which in turn helps to create the cultures they build. Adding the personal dimension to your culture build will inspire others to also consider their whys and reasons for committing their time and energies to the cause. Being authentic is binding.

Sales is not a straightforward business; it is really a multifaceted profession. It's not only about information gathering, data analysis, and problem solving, but also fundamentally about helping to make a difference. It is also about managing and developing people, yourself included. When spinning multiple plates, it is easy to get drawn into specifics or details. The tools and approaches I will outline are also about giving you the space and the perspective to keep your eyes on the prize, allowing you to drive the inputs of your business toward achieving your goals.

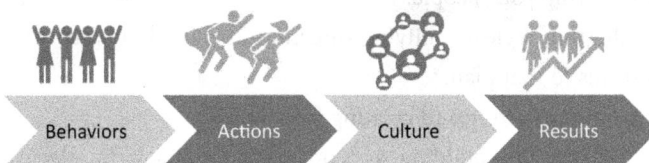

Figure F.1 Behaviors form culture leading to results

When we think of people in this context, it is everyone you come into contact with: your customers most importantly, your team, your leadership, and your cross-functional colleagues. If you harness the power of people and bind them to a mission, there is nothing at all that you cannot achieve together.

I was, as I am sure many are, promoted to sales leadership and management without training or previous experience. I remember immediately trying to find resources to help guide me. A quick Internet search on this topic today will pull back plenty on a host of related subjects, usually bullet points focusing on the human skill elements of sales leadership, how to deal with difficult people or situations, how to hone an elevator pitch, how to manage a pipeline, and how great leaders approach their world and show up every day. That's all very useful. However, still to this day, I struggle to find a comprehensive and practical guide as to how to pull all these elements together.

What is also to my mind missing is the critical role cultural leadership plays in successful sales organizations. Unfortunately, it is altogether more usual for us to remember organizations where the leadership or go-to market propositions were dysfunctional, than it is to remember leadership and commercial organizations that were truly united, and which truly hummed.

There are, however, outstanding examples, which all have a number of common threads, which is what I have attempted to capture in this book, or at least within an approach which has delivered long-term growth for me throughout my career in sales. Key to this journey will be several fundamental milestones; what I will do is center and deliver insights aimed at these, always in the context of people-first culture building.

The Layering Process

1. Understanding your business and what the data is telling you.
2. Knowing your people.
3. Charting a clear, unifying direction and binding your people and teams to that plan.
4. Communicating and creating followership.
5. Shaping and building a people-first approach to executing and winning, not just once but consistently.

6. Highlighting and building behaviors which become the backbone to your culture.
7. Focusing as much on your three- to five-year plan as you are on the current challenges of the present financial year.
8. Knowing and managing yourself within a growth mindset.
9. Knowing your values and attributes on the pathway to developing your leadership brand.

A Universal Approach

I have been lucky enough to work in multiple industries and across multiple geographies. The tenets of setting a direction, forming a culture, maintaining that culture, making a living plan, reviewing, pivoting, communicating, hiring, and developing employees are all constant.

They are universal, regardless of sector or whether you are at a multinational company or at a startup. I aim therefore to create a book for all sales leaders no matter where they are on their leadership journey or sector, regardless of the solutions they serve or sell.

Why Write This Book?

While many organizations now focus on developing their identified talent, not all are effectively making course material or learnings readily available to employees. I was talking to a founder of a training/coaching company recently, who suggested that less than 25 percent of the companies he engages with had any formal learning budget or agenda, and therefore confirmed that the promotion without training model is still very much alive and well.

> *Most newly promoted leaders don't receive leadership training. They are left to their own devices from the beginning and the myth that being a good leader is an inborn quality is perpetuated.*
> —Taken from *Bankable Leadership* by Dr. Tasha Eurich.
> Copyright © 2013 by Dr. Tasha. Used by permission of the author. www.tashaeurich.com.

Another observation throughout my career is that very few organizations give their management a pause or a time-out to consider and reflect on their leadership journeys and all too many of us are working week by week in the moment, striving to achieve the outcomes of our businesses. It is important to schedule time to learn the lessons that will help you improve, and to help you make the greatest impacts on your team through its culture.

The drive to focus on the day by day can often come from the very top of the organization. Sales leadership, and executing a mature, focused go-to market approach, is a discipline all of its own and should be recognized as such. It is not unusual for senior leadership to be setting an agenda and go-to market approach that reflects their own skills and knowledge centers, whether this be a finance, accountancy, or a founder sensibility. Founder cultures can be great examples of this, whereby a fabulous, charismatic, visionary salesperson leading a company may not themselves have the ability to think beyond how they personally approach the role. Activity, activity, activity without guidance and focus can lead to chaos.

As such, communication and binding senior leaders to an aligned approach and strategy to be pursued, is an enormously important component of being a people-first sales leader. It is also vital to then focus on and police the approach, especially in challenging environments, in order to ensure that the go-to market does not unintentionally become chaotic once more.

You must ensure that your senior management understands and is as bought into the mission as your team is. Followership and culture building goes two ways: internally as well as externally through the approaches you take to market. The support, investment, and, sometimes, aircover of your leaders and your fellow cross-functional colleagues are therefore a vital component to your potential long-term success. This also ensures that good ideas are encouraged and can come from anywhere in the organization, as all have a unified understanding and mission around winning in market.

I therefore want to share templates and approaches which can help you create and share your strategy and approach. That can, medium to long term, afford you the time to review, pivot, and then think beyond your current financial year. Learning and self-reflection should not be consigned to the annual review process. These templates will build to the tools I used to formulate vision, direction, purpose, and approach in the formulation of culture, and that allowed me to receive action-focused feedback along the way. They can become tools which are the living backbone of your performance engine.

Creating a winning culture is the key to sustained and exponential growth at any organization; it is the magic dust that many organizations struggle to attain. You do not achieve it overnight. You must actively focus on it and never take it for granted once you have it.

A Word on Making It Your Own

Everything can of course be improved upon. My hope is to pass on some ideas that help to structure your approach. Do bear in mind that as with anything, the key is to make things your own and to bring yourself authentically to whatever you do.

Do not, I ask you, use any of these suggestions as simply templates to execute against. I have witnessed this and while you can succeed, it will not, on its own, produce the exponential growth you are seeking. Just as you will ask others to think creatively about your business, so you should challenge yourself to do likewise.

Consider where you are on your personal journey in sales leadership. What are your strengths and weaknesses? Seek inputs from others and consider where you need help or support. You must bring yourself authentically to the process and build upon what I present. Do allow yourself time to think creatively about what your data is telling you and where you can take your business; it's your creative inputs and your instincts that will elevate what I present to the next level.

Please adapt what you find to the sensibilities of your business, your geography, and your industry, which only you can be expert in. Also be attendant to your personality, strengths, and approaches. Make everything your own. You, alongside your people, are the force multiplier.

Thanks

I cannot proceed any further without a heartfelt thank you to those who have supported and shaped me in business and life over the years. My sincere and heartfelt thanks go out to family, and to those business and sales leaders who have left me better than when they first met me. Also to the many colleagues who have made this career journey so complete and so much fun. Sales has enabled me to see the world and to live and work within the most diverse cultures and groups. It has forever enriched me as a person and developed me far beyond my meager talents.

My deepest thanks go to those who have supported, developed, and believed in me across all facets of my life. You all know who you are and there are too many to mention. Sales is the ultimate people business; many of you have become my closest friends and I always look forward to our meetings across the world over a cocktail or great meal—here's to many more of those!

Takeaways

- *As a sales leader, you are there to develop, nurture, and grow your portfolio; if you see this in profit and loss (P&L) terms alone, you will miss so much potential to grow something transformational.*
- *Identify those you can learn from and find your values and your sales philosophy.*
- *Unleash the talents of your people by developing, nurturing, and growing them.*
- *Making it your own, bringing yourself authentically and creatively to the mission, and binding all with you will add an injection of rocket fuel to your plans.*
- *Think in terms of how to lift your planning and thinking beyond your current financial year.*

CHAPTER 1

Introduction

Chapter Summary

- Consider the transformational benefits of a people-first approach to sales leadership.
- Make your people your force multiplier when fused to your go-to market strategy.
- Create behaviors which service your KPIs and metrics rather than relying solely on these metrics to drive your people.
- Always be authentic in your leadership style.
- Focus on creating behaviors which will solidify into culture.

I am a lifelong salesperson. This is a book about sales leadership, creating a performance culture and followership. It is about creating a vision and then building an organization and approach, which will make that vision a reality. It's about building a people-first culture that is bound to the vision you have set out, and it is about thinking beyond the present to where you want to be as an organization in three- to five-year's time.

What Is a "People-First" Culture and What Impacts Can It Deliver?

A people-first culture is one that prioritizes the well-being, development, and satisfaction of its team members above all else. The reason I am emphasizing the importance of culture build within sales leadership is that this approach over others can have several transformational and positive effects within any organization:

1. *Increased morale and engagement*: When employees feel that their well-being and needs are a top priority, they are more likely to be authentically engaged and motivated. They feel valued, appreciated,

and invested in. This in turn builds morale and commitment to the team and the organization.

2. *Stronger team cohesion*: A people-first culture fosters a sense of belonging and camaraderie across team members and across organizational functions. When individuals feel supported, cared for, and heard, they are more likely to collaborate effectively and build stronger relationships within and across teams.

3. *Enhanced communication*: Open and honest communication is a hallmark of people-first cultures. Team members are encouraged to express and share their ideas, concerns, and feedback without fear. Such transparency leads to better communications within the team aligned to the goals of the company.

4. *Improved retention and talent acquisition*: Organizations that prioritize their employees' well-being tend to have lower turnover rates, as people who feel that their personal and professional needs are being met have less reason to look elsewhere. It also helps to attract new talent through personal recommendations and good reviews (such as Glassdoor) in the market. Remember, in sales, your folks have developed networks and it is highly likely that they will frequently meet the competition across the course of a year at various events. Become the workplace your competitors want to work at.

5. *Higher productivity and creativity*: Employees in people-first cultures are more likely to bring their full selves to work, which leads to greater creativity and innovation. They are also more bonded to the mission, meaning they are more likely to go that extra mile in achieving team and organizational goals.

6. *Better problem solving*: In an environment where team members are valued and encouraged to be heard, problem solving becomes more effective. Diverse opinions are welcomed, often leading to more comprehensive and creative solutions, usually and critically, with more widespread buy-in.

7. *Reduced stress and burnout*: Prioritizing the well-being of the team can help to reduce stress and prevent burnout. When backed by resources and support, they will also feel better equipped to manage the challenges of their roles.

8. *Positive impact on performance metrics*: Organizations with a people-first culture often see great improvements in key performance metrics such as customer satisfaction, sales, profitability, and great places to work surveys.

To my mind, you cannot do any of these things effectively unless you are interested in people. Sales, and especially sales leadership, is about caring for people. It is, by definition, a people business:

> *Sales leadership is about being authentically people-first in mindset and execution.*

People, passion, and product are the secret sauce of any successful enterprise. Of course, not every sales culture or leader is wired to operate with, as opposed to through, their people. I have been in process-driven cultures driven by metrics, money-driven cultures, and target-driven cultures. These very outcome-orientated organizations tend to live month by month, quarter by quarter, and year by year. You will also see a lot of employee turnover and burnout along the way. Numbers become the driving force, as opposed to destination-driven goals and subsequently, leaders can become data rather than people orientated. To bind and build culture in a more human-centric fashion, use metrics as tools, not goals.

Why Focus on Being People-First?

People are often referred to as the "lifeblood" of an organization or sales team because they play a central role in its functioning and success. Consider the impacts they could be making within a shift to a more people-centric approach:

1. *Drive and energy*: People bring motivation and enthusiasm to the workplace. Unlocking their passion, dedication, and creativity is essential for driving any organization forward and to it realizing its goals.
2. *Problem solving*: You cannot do it all alone, nor should you try. Leaders who constantly provide answers and direction are not developing

trust or independence. Allow your people to identify challenges and generate innovative solutions and adaptations.

3. *Customer relationships*: In sales, building and maintaining relationships is crucial. People are vital for understanding client needs and delivering value.

4. *Collaboration*: Teamwork is essential for real success. If your team is collaborating, sharing ideas, and working together to achieve commonly understood objectives, your whole organization will become more effective.

5. *Innovation*: People can bring fresh perspectives and creativity if allowed to, provided that they are shown the expectation to deliver in this way within a psychologically safe environment. Innovations can shape product, marketing, process improvements and go-to market enhancements.

6. *Adaptation*: People are not one-trick ponies. People have the ability to pivot, learn new skills, and adjust to evolving circumstances, if supported and aligned to a mission.

7. *Leadership*: You will find your leaders of tomorrow within your cohort to support, motivate, and focus everyone on the commonly aligned goals.

8. *Culture shapers*: The collective behavior, values, and attitudes of employees will shape the organizational culture. A positive winning culture can both engage and attract talent.

9. *Customer obsession*: Happy and engaged employees are more likely to advocate for enhanced products and services, which can lead to positive word of mouth marketing, partnership, and reputation in the market.

10. *Ownership and responsibility*: Individuals taking ownership of their roles and responsibility for actions, outcomes, and results, will drive you toward your goals faster.

11. *Human connection*: Bringing your teams together helps to build trust, rapport, empathy, and alignment across departments toward shared goals and sets of outcomes.

There are always extremes. Early in my career, straight out of university, I worked for bosses who literally threw sports car keys on the board room table and drove a performance culture solely toward the attainment of wealth. It was actually a real-life example of the Ben Affleck scene in *Boiler Room*. *Boiler Room* and *Glengarry Glen Ross* are two of the most outstanding sales movies ever made, focusing on the "ABC" (always be closing) approach to sales, which maximizes the number and minimizes the individual, often at any costs. *Mad Men* is brilliant as well for the art of the value-based sales approaches, but, again, celebrates the talented, driven, often flawed individual. Of course, there is dramatic tension built in, but all of the aforementioned depict aspects of sales and salespeople which are often very true and mostly singular in approach. I am sure all, within a sales career, over time, will recognize traits and aspects from these works of fiction. I have literally lived scenes from all three. There is, however, a better way than the singular approaches portrayed in these works of art. Working together as one team, aligned to the goal, is where success, joy, and excitement really kicks in.

Metrics and Key Performance Indicators (KPIs)

Metrics and KPIs are without doubt an attendant part of any sales function. Which ones are selected and how they are used to drive things, even when certain metrics are used, can have a real impact on the cultural environment, as they show what is uppermost in the sales leader's mind.

While on the face of it funnel metrics such as number of e-mails, calls, meetings, and proposals can certainly drive activity, the danger of such an approach that defines "x" number of calls => "x" number of meetings => "x" number of proposals and "x" number of sales can often drive activity for activity's sakes. What you do not want is people working to the metrics as opposed to people thinking and acting creatively about their businesses.

Instead of bringing a thoughtful approach to market, representatives can end up adapting themselves purely to the metrics and not transformational outcomes. This can also happen with purely quota- or target-driven companies. I have worked for leaders who were status driven, managing up while directing their reports with no interest in them beyond their quotas—business all the time, every conversation opening with, "what have you got for me?" type approaches, married to what I would characterize as a "pipeline jockey" method of leadership. If you are working in this type of environment, ask yourself if you have seen or if you understand what the go-to market strategy is. Likely as not, there is not one. This standoffish type of approach leaves so much opportunity on the table as salespeople are essentially left to their own devices in terms of the opportunities discussed in the pipeline calls.

Pipelines, again, are super important, of course, and tell you so much about the state and direction of the business, but if you are simply looking at the one data set alone, without consideration to strategic, structured approaches to market and considering as well other commercial levers, then you are never going to make a full mark on the business. We will look into the data and insights that can drive your strategy at length later, but if you are not setting a strategy that breaks your market opportunity down, and thinks about where it is focusing and what its priorities are, then you are planning to fail.

Make metrics tools, not goals. I prefer, for example, to confer on the sales team the role of customer and market expertise. I expect them to know their businesses, including where and how to play, while ensuring there are enough "coffee and cocktails," or meaningful customer interactions happening all the time. If you show that what you take seriously is customer interaction, for example, you are more likely to bed down a behavior that sticks organizationally. Instead of driving through a metric, you have then embedded a behavior from which culture can grow.

Sales strategy is about widely understood laser focuses. You cannot focus and finish if everyone is shooting for everything and are more concerned to hit call, meeting, and proposal metrics. It is shocking to me how some highly regarded organizations grow and become highly lauded when actually there is no defined strategic go-to market plan at all. Dig a little deeper and you can soon find that the pipeline is full of more dirt than diamonds. You may even find this is true of the existing customer base as well. Ensuring your team takes on the responsibility of expertise while binding them to a mission allows for more creative expression and overall better outcomes—long term.

Founder cultures can also be challenging, where the magic and single-mindedness of the entrepreneur can actually help to create chaos or, worst, does not allow for alternative points of view or oversight into strategy or approach. I have witnessed both, where the charisma of the founder pulls all energy and efforts toward their ever-changing focuses and where a world-beating proposition has ultimately failed because practical approaches to development or tech have not been taken in the pursuit of unachievable perfection. It can also be where hiring in the founder's image has engrained the chaos, often combined with convoluted reporting structures, ensuring that the company gets in its own way more often than not in the pursuit of its revenue goals.

If your goal is to build something sustainable, something that will continuously grow, then a perspective switch from purely focusing on the signed contract versus focusing on your people and how they go about their business is key. This is not to diminish ambition or aggression in the market at all; these are necessary components. We are here to win for our companies at the end of the day, but it is to accept the position that the true differentiator in your business is your people and that anything can be achieved by a united, focused team having fun in the pursuit of aligned goals. Organizations that focus only on the sales numbers and metrics truly miss out on a force multiplier on the road to sustainable exponential growth. This is about obsessively focusing on clear objectives matched to a support of the folks affecting change for your business.

Counterbalancing any negative experiences of sales or business leadership has been experiences of working with and for the most inspirational people and culture builders—super ambitious but also focused first on the people around them and laying those bricks with care and attention while building repeatably growing, sustainably forward-looking organizations. If there is one magic ingredient, it has to be authentic people-first leadership. That is what this book is about.

Embedding Behaviors Which Create Culture

Behaviors are key to building culture. A proactive approach to shaping behaviors within a team that aligns with KPIs and metrics, rather than relying solely on these metrics to drive people, is going to fast track to a sustainable culture build. Take a deliberate approach to cultivating behaviors that naturally contribute to achieving organizational goals. Here are some considerations to help support creating behaviors that serve your KPIs and metrics:

1. *Define desired behaviors*: Clearly articulate the specific behaviors that align with the achievement of your KPIs and metrics. These could include qualities like collaboration, innovation, customer focus, and efficiency.
2. *Communicate expectations*: Use clear examples and case studies of how behaviors have positively impacted your business.
3. *Provide resources and support*: Equip your team with the necessary resources and support to exhibit the desired behaviors. This could involve training, mentorship, access to tools, or any other elements that facilitate the development of these behaviors.
4. *Link behaviors to values*: Connect the desired behaviors to the core values of the organization. This helps in establishing a strong cultural foundation and reinforces the importance of these behaviors in the larger context.
5. *Encourage ownership*: Foster a sense of ownership among team members. When individuals feel a personal stake in the success of the organization, they are more likely to adopt behaviors that contribute to achieving KPIs.
6. *Recognize and reward*: Acknowledge and reward individuals who consistently demonstrate the desired behaviors. Recognition can be a powerful motivator and reinforces the link between behaviors and positive outcomes.
7. *Promote cross-functional collaboration*: Many KPIs involve multiple facets of the business. Encourage behaviors that support collaboration across different teams and departments to ensure a holistic approach to achieving goals.
8. *Provide feedback and coaching*: Regularly provide constructive feedback on behaviors. Offer coaching and mentorship to help individuals improve and develop the skills and attitudes that align with your KPIs.
9. *Adjust and adapt*: Be open to adjusting the identified behaviors based on feedback and changing business needs. Flexibility is crucial in responding to evolving circumstances.

10. *Lead by example*: Leadership sets the tone for the entire organization. Leaders should consistently exhibit the desired behaviors, reinforcing their importance through actions as well as words.

By actively shaping behaviors that naturally contribute to the achievement of KPIs and metrics, you create a culture where success becomes an inherent part of the way your team operates. It's a proactive way to align your team to the broader goals of the business.

Authentic Leadership

For me, this is about being not only customer obsessed—focused—but also aware of one's limitations and weaknesses. The sense that it takes a village, and the more diverse that company, provided that they are aligned, the better and more powerful the unit will become. Authentic leaders are interested in their people and in helping them to be better through creating safe environments for them to express themselves and succeed.

Authentic leaders listen more and direct less. They encourage dialogue and ideas. This, alongside a conferred trust through enablement, is how a psychologically safe environment is created, where your people can express themselves and solve their own challenges, while being closely bonded to the mission. Authentic leaders are also honest about what they do not know. They are confident in the knowledge that expertise exists around them and that the job is to free the organization to be able to work as best it can. The most authentic leaders often speak in terms of getting out of their team's way and focusing on allowing them to be as successful as they can be.

None of this is to say that nothing can be escalated or discussed, but it is to say that the emphasis is on the team to have thought through possible solutions before issues are presented for decision making. It is also, as we will cover in later sections, about being focused on the longer term, not constantly eyes down in the battle for the outcomes of the current financial year—instead, creating an environment where looking around corners and to the three- to five-year plan is as important.

Authentic leadership allows you to be focused not just on the current year and challenges.

I have witnessed too many sales organizations that are living very much in the moment, day to day, month by month, quarter by quarter. In that type of environment, there is altogether too much learning in the moment, which usually means learning by mistakes. Don't get me wrong; there will always be mistakes and losses. While this is often the best way to learn, I want to share some ideas and principles that can help to fast track transformational outcomes and performance. When this is not in place, it is all too common to see companies who frequently have to pivot, or restructure, because the leadership feels that the salesforce is failing or believes that new blood is the only answer.

It is my conclusion, therefore, that if your leadership style is not people-first in focus, you will most likely have a culture that celebrates individualism and will ultimately struggle to attract and or retain people in the long run. It is likely that in those organizations, the eyes are down, the pressure is on, and there is little in the way of looking around corners and into the future of the company. You can expect boom and bust in such environments and for the daily pressures to take their toll eventually. As a result, when interviewing, I always ask about the culture of the company I am considering. This is a question you should corroborate from multiple sources and viewpoints, as cultures can often be stated as opposed to actually lived and breathed.

That's also a consideration to ask those who you are asking to join your enterprise. Let's be clear that culture does not have to be perfect or yet fully evolved. I love and respect leaders who will tell you upfront where they think they are failing or where the organization needs focus or help. If the culture or performance is not what is desired, I also look for any insights into what the existing leadership style is and the goals and ambitions this group has set for establishing or maintaining a performance-led culture.

If you are entering a business that has issues, it is important to know that your values are aligned to those above you and that, in working together toward the agreed goals, you will have support and backing to effect the changes you need to. Much of this could also be about maturity—in other words, the point in the developmental journey of the company. This, again, can be a facet of a founder-based culture or start-up scene, where pure hustle needs to mature into service delivery and expansion plans for existing clients over time. It does not matter if the company acknowledges that it is at a certain stage of maturity, for example, a start-up, or if cultural elements are not yet attained, as long as it is acknowledged that elements are lacking, with a stated ambition to build something sustainable and future focused over time.

It is for this reason that turnaround situations and business-building opportunities are therefore some of the most compelling situations for a sales leader to enter, as you have a canvass on which to create the vision, culture, and goals that you will travel toward as one group. You do, however, always need the buy-in of your leadership group and senior management. Make sure they are not the ones driving some of these existing cultural issues. If they are, use the templates and approaches outlined throughout this book to build toward a consensus view on the approach to market using data- and insight-driven strategy building.

Like any career in sales, I have had high highs and some major lows. I have been in some truly toxic environments and a few exceptional ones. All of it is a learning journey. Over time, I have developed my approach and philosophy of sales along with strategies for building successful winning teams. This book investigates those processes, offering insights into the approaches and templates that have proven effective for me. All that is contained within, this book, has served me well across my career. My hope and aspiration is that the content within these pages can offer meaningful value to individuals considering a career in sales or for those navigating various stages in the profession.

If there is one clear encapsulation of what I am trying to lay out here, it comes from one of the best leaders I have worked for, a dear friend and remarkable human. He would always speak in terms of:

> *Behaviors form culture leading to results.*

I firmly believe in this mantra. I was struck, when first hearing this, by the simplicity of the statement and reflected that unconsciously this is what I had been doing in creating and leading teams throughout my career. My good friend has made a successful career of executing this approach at an organizational level, yielding incredible and exponential results in revenue wherever he has gone. Working in my friend's organizations was always hard work and passionate, but always so much fun.

Revenue was not all he was delivering. By living this mantra, he was also delivering culture which, in turn, bred excitement and joy to be working together successfully toward a common goal. No surprise then that the organizations he has built have been where people have most wanted to work. He has gained followership and a global bench of talent who would love to come join him, whatever his next venture might be— organizations in which you can see, feel, and measure your impact as well as your own personal growth.

Being people-first is very much about fundamentally helping people while simultaneously allowing them to express themselves in an open and psychologically safe environment. I love this statement as well (another one of his), not only because I have lived it and recognize it in practice, but because it speaks to personal responsibility and the setting of a vision.

It is also ultimately about getting the people side right. If you get the people right, you will succeed; the results will come because there is nothing you cannot achieve with a group of diverse and talented individuals joined together in the execution of a plan they all buy into.

My goal, therefore, in this book is to focus on the elements that help you to build a sustained and successful sales engine and culture. I am not interested, nor am I focused on what you might call the year-to-year survival method of sales leadership. This is a book about avoiding boom and bust, firefighting, and constant escalation of issues. This is about creating an engine that hums and allows you to look around the corners you are approaching, as well as plan for the future.

If you think of organizational leadership in terms of maturity, this end state is also the time when you can consider your company fully formed, as you will have a functioning, performing team and your leadership discussions will be elevated to more strategic goals and deliverables. The journey does not stop here, however, as neglected teams fail, cultures are not permanent, and you are only ever one bad hire or head-hunter away from a retention issue. As such, think of sales leadership as an ongoing exercise, one you should always vigilantly have your eye on and one where your job is never truly done.

What needs to be true to win?

This is a concept we will return to again and again across the piece. Always be asking this question and instill this ethos across your teams. Think of this as also about establishing your brand as a sales leader and creating buy-in and followership around your organization. This is as much about investment in your organization as it is about you. Think about what you need to win as well

Takeaways

- *A people-first culture can be transformational.*
- *Consider why a people-first approach could best support your go-to market success.*
- *Building a winning culture takes time and is a layering process.*
- *Define the behaviors and values, including your own, that you want to see in your group.*
- *Authentically tie your leadership style to your values and what you consider to be the most important.*
- *Be watchful and vigilant toward your built culture; your job is never done.*

CHAPTER 2

The Stages of Sales Management

Chapter Summary

- There are distinct stages of sales leadership; be aware of the unique challenges you face in each one.
- Do not obsess on what you do not know; consider instead what got you to where you are and what you need to make the next steps in your leadership journey.
- Remember, your challenges are not unique and you are not alone.
- Use tools and techniques that allow you to collate and use data on your business to decide where to focus for maximum impact.

Whether you are newly promoted to lead a sales team or entering into a new organization to set the goals and agenda, the grace period is usually small. There will, of course, be a honeymoon period, which is important to maximize. During this period, absorb all you can and use the general goodwill toward your appointment to ask as many questions as you can, as well as to understand the current business focuses.

While it is tempting, launching headlong into the job is not likely to be a strategy that will pay off. Perhaps, in the short term, you will see a fresh impetus and energy, but if you are not assessing and planning where to focus your efforts on building something fresh, you will not be affecting any substantive change compared to what went on before you took over the reins.

In this instance, should current results persist, you will likely find yourself under pressure sooner than you would like to be, which will only draw you deeper in the minutia of the day-to-day firefighting. It should be noted, however, that it is often hard to not be sucked into the day-to-day detail straight off the bat. This is particularly true if you are also learning a new business or industry, or if your business or markets are complex. The sense of drinking from a hose can further panic you to spend more and more time in the trenches, as you are purely conscious of what you don't know as opposed to why you are there.

This is why it is vital to take some time to consider what you are stepping into, as well as to consider what is really important and to distill these thoughts using tools and structures, which will allow you to make sense of all the competing calls for your time.

Let's take a moment to focus on that sensation of not being expert. I would advise you to quickly become comfortable in what you don't know; remember, you were hired for what you do know. There will come pressures for sure; some folks will expect you to fix all their product issues, while others may even use a lack of expertise in industry terms to undermine you. None of this truly matters when you can help to transform an organization through its people and focuses. This is where you should focus your mind and your priorities. This is the greatest impact you can bring. There will be plenty of experts in the business and you will learn over time. Be on the lookout for where there is complexity which is getting in the way of the organization and create clear narratives for ways to cut through and improve. Understand your organization and its go-to market intimately. Where to play, how to win, and what needs to be true to win are critical for you to become intimate with, above all else.

The First Sales Management Appointment

I, like many, first tasted the experience of sales management when I was promoted from within my existing team. I was young, the most recent hire, and thoroughly inexperienced in terms of people management. I was also, at the time, the best performer across the group.

The qualities I had brought to my individual sales role were curiosity and a desire to always improve my value proposition to clients. I naturally built bridges to win. I interacted with colleagues in support and implementation and I naturally considered all customer-facing operations as part of one culture. I would habitually seek out and identify those in the organization who were expert, or what I considered as successful, and would spend time with them to learn from, then adapt my approach to make my own style toward the customers.

I was certainly successful, but I was not attuned as to why those qualities had garnered me the promotion. This meant that I was nervous and unsure of myself when taking on the role. I did not fully appreciate the change of perspective needed to lead a team. I was always very conscious of the changed relationship with my peers. I was most certainly acting in a real sense as opposed to fully inhabiting my role. In retrospect, I threw myself in and brought more energy than I did critical analysis to the job. I had a level of expertise in selling complex solutions and this is what carried me through. We were very much living one financial year to another prior to my appointment, and I have to admit, post my appointment as well. I was as well managing some of the most singular individuals I have ever experienced in my career and it took me over a year to ask my management for any training to support my development in the role, largely because I felt that I had to "earn my strips" before making asks for investment.

It is impossible not to spare a few words about single contributors at this point. A single contributor is an individual who helps a company toward its goals without management responsibility. Single-contribution roles are vital in the context of business and often include an element of expertise. In the context of my career journey at the point when I was promoted, I was indeed a single contributor in my role as a business development manager. The challenge I now faced was that I had to develop skills beyond my single-contribution level. Yes, I could share the sales techniques and approaches which had made me successful and thereby support a widening of this type of opportunity across the group, but I was also very much acting like the player manager as opposed to setting a vision and building a comprehensive approach to market beneath this. I was, therefore, doing nothing to dramatically change the culture of the team beyond its collective of other single contributors such as myself.

There is another meaning to the term single contributor that we should also investigate. The term can also be used to denote the style of approach an individual takes to their business or function in less desirable terms. It can have a negative context in as much as single contributors can be just that, utterly singular in personality and approach. The fact that they are often successful also conveys on them a license to continue to act in ways that are not always conducive to building a team or even a consistent business.

This could be manifested in a number of ways: weaponizing information, tightly holding onto customers, openly criticizing other functions or cutting across organizational lines, or established processes of operating, in order to prioritize their initiatives over others. In leadership terms, it can also come in the form of what I would term "highly directive" as opposed to people management styles. A direction-led leader is more likely to emphasize activity while telling folks what they should be doing and where they should be focusing, as opposed to helping their team or individuals develop their own solutions and approaches while acting in support of them. There is an implicit lack of trust in the relationship. If the numbers are not there, then the team is inherently failing. There is often no sense of helping to define use-cases and winning approaches to market to help their folks to focus in order to win.

It can be a real double-edged sword. In both senses, salespeople are (not exclusively, but...) often seen as the ultimate single contributors in an organization. Great salespeople know where and how to hunt, they know how to shape a proposition to a client's need, they know what it takes to win, and they thrive on this. They are also incentivized and motivated by the win; commission is a lifeblood. As such, some can be entirely deal focused to the determent of all else. They are myopically focused on the win and do not care what it takes or what relationships are burnt on the way to victory. These individuals can find it hard to share, to acknowledge a lack of expertise, and to train or coach others and yet, if they are consistently finding and closing business, their influence can be seen to be greater than their actual impact on the business and its culture.

You certainly do need these heroes in your team and business. The challenge may come when single contribution becomes single minded of thought and action or if they are perceived to be treated as differently to others, provided more leeway, and so on. It can also impact an organization if the resultant wins require too much customization or are not aligned to product or strategy and if these come at all costs, then tensions can certainly occur within the wider business.

A conundrum can occur for any sales leader if a high-revenue contributor is also a throttle on other colleagues or supporting functions and ultimately impacts the culture. Such figures can also react poorly to new approaches, ideas, and the suggestion of collaboration. At worst, they can jealously hold onto knowledge and expertise as if it is an intellectual property (IP) to their very success. This dynamic can often be most clearly seen in the management of key strategic accounts and leads to the phenomenon of bowtie versus diamond thinking when it comes to these. (We will discuss this at length later.)

As pointed out, it should also be recognized that single contributors and successful salespeople do not always make the best people managers and yet sometimes, as a factor of their success, it is assumed that they can also thrive as leaders. Success as a sales person does not automatically confer success as a sales manager. These are very different disciplines, though clearly, they are deeply connected. All this being true, it happens again and again. The simple expectation is that whatever gold dust that makes you successful will naturally soon cover the team. Makes sense right? The best salesperson should transform a sales team. Wrong.

Going back to my first appointment as a sales manager, I was also dealing with a number of these personalities and suddenly that day I found that my world had changed completely. As a high-performing sales executive, I was now thrust into managing and being responsible for a team of colleagues who now viewed and perceived me very differently than before. I also inherited a sales plan that I could not find, as it was not articulated anywhere. A consideration that had not troubled me before as a single contributor!

It was no longer only all about me and my individual performance, essentially solving my client's needs. Now I had to contend with a whole new set of dynamics ranging from the expectations of my management, to the need to build a very different type of relationship with those who perceived themselves, quite rightly, as more senior and more experienced than I was at the time.

You also have to consider your senior management in this as well. I think, in retrospect, they preferred to deal with me than some of these more contentious personalities in terms of day-to-day management of the business, in effect throwing me the hospital pass to sort things out. As I felt that these were my issues to resolve and came with the role, I did not discuss with them or align on what we wanted to achieve culturally beyond the numbers. Maybe I projected it or maybe it was real, but there seemed to suddenly be a wall between me and the team. Caution, perhaps fear or suspicion, and maybe even resentment were the new shifting sands I would have to navigate.

I was very nervous about what I perceived to be my knowledge gaps. This is a fear that can often inhibit us enormously and sometimes those around us might be using this to their advantage or we might be obsessing about the perception we are showing others if we fall down on technical details, or on the minutia of the product. Every now and again in your career, you will come across folks who will test you on this, trying to show you up for what you do not know. It is important here to be confident about and know what your knowledge gaps and limitations are. You do not have to know everything. That is why you have experts in your business and diverse teams to work with after all. Saying you do not know and asking questions is not a weakness.

Had I had access to the perspectives and tools we will cover in subsequent chapters, I would have been able to better organize my thoughts, control my emotions, and focus on data-influenced priorities, thereby radically dialing down the pressure on myself, allowing for a confident approach to communicate our priorities to the team and the business. I would have been able to build culture as opposed to serving the embedded way of things.

It was clear to me that my management was trying to change the dynamic of the company and trying to inject fresh impetus into the team, but in lifting me up, they also left me feeling both isolated and out of my depth. It was not all about the team either; your executive relationships have also changed and I certainly did not identify at the time that I needed to consider my communication and visibility as much as I needed to lead the team.

I was too inexperienced to ask for help, feeling that I should "earn my spurs" before asking for investment in my development. Hardly anyone in this example is being offered training or support to change from a matter expertise as a salesperson to a people leader. Unfortunately, this is why so many fail. Leadership can be learnt but it is not always an innate quality.

If you find yourself in this position, remember, your experiences are actually more common than you think. Also focus on the fact that others have believed in you to change the bigger picture. The truth is you are never alone, but when thrust into this position, it is hard not to feel that your situation is utterly unique to you and that you are isolated. It was assumed that I would thrive, yet I had no mentor or coach. Over time, I would find these resources and support. I would also ask for investment in my training, but to begin with, all I felt was that I carried the full burden of expectation.

So, in conclusion, it is often assumed that the best salesperson would be able to turnaround the sales team. Often, the answer to that is no. Often, that newly promoted hire will bounce out of the company within six months to a year, if not able to adapt. This is actually a very common experience, particularly in companies where the overall strategy is perhaps not well articulated. It is not the only scenario you will face as a sales leader, however;

Transforming Existing Organizations

As your career develops, you will find that you are hired or asked to build or transform teams. The hiring of an experienced sales leader from the market either coincides with a moment of the company's maturity and growth, or heralds an acknowledgment that what has gone before has not served the needs and ambitions of the company. It could also be once a start-up has reached a moment of needing to mature its approaches and methods, or it could be at an established company where growth has stalled.

Sometimes, it is because something has been going wrong, people have left; the management feels that the potential has not been realized or, worse, a total reset is required. You might even be hired to be told in your interviews that there are people or dynamics that "you will need to fix or solve for." As already pointed out, teams and cultures if not maintained and nurtured can easily decline or collapse. It is also true that in cultures that are not working, disruptive forces can be at play or even encouraged whether willingly or unwillingly.

What is common to all these scenarios is that it is often hard to find anything that provides you a base from which to go about your new role. The number of times I have asked for or looked for the previous strategy or sales plan and found little or nothing is telling. Do not let this concern you; this is actually the best environment for you to effect fundamental and lasting change through setting and communicating a plan to which you will bind the organization.

The first thing that should tell you that a plan is absent is the behaviors and conversations of the people in the business across its functions. You can also sense this in the behaviors of the salespeople. Good salespeople are rightly expert, but if that projected expertise does not marry to the quality or consistency of onboarded customers, then something else is at play. A great idea when entering a situation like this is to focus as much on the customers as your inherited team. Are the deals being won the right deals? Are they profitable? Is there a discerned strategy at play or is it a scattergun approach to market?

As you spend time in the business, sales meetings, sales kick-offs, leadership forums, and the like will also give you plenty of insights. What is the organization spending its time debating? If the topics are consistently getting into the weeds and minutia of product, then you might find this confusion mirrored in where best to prospect and close in the market. This type of noise can be deafening unless clarity, prioritization, and focus are brought to bear.

So, the management has decided to change the course by appointing a new sales leader. Many factors can be at play in pitching a company into this need to reset and find new purpose and direction. Ultimately, it can come down to the pressure to perform. So many organizations are running to meet their budgets and it is because, unfortunately, it is all too easy to get caught up into firefighting, chasing all opportunity or worst, that some fall into instincts of micro management and directive leadership. Suddenly, as a result, all morale and purpose in a unit can quickly dissipate. On the face of it, you're told something simple: turn around the team, they are not addressing the opportunity in the market. Turn around implies a simple change of direction. Recognize, however, that a successful transformation goes beyond a mere change in personnel or direction; it necessitates a comprehensive analysis of the factors contributing to the current performance.

Rather than a hasty opting for a new course, a strategic and thorough examination of the underlying issues is imperative, if you want to make lasting change. This involves becoming the detective to meticulously review the existing strategies, internal processes, and external influences on the commercial business. By delving deep into the root causes of the current challenges, commercial leaders can gain valuable insights that inform a nuanced and effective turnaround strategy. Only through thoughtful scrutiny and a layering approach to covering the groundwork can a resilient and sustainable transformation be charted.

You should, therefore, be conscious of and jealous of your time. Meetings for meeting's sake, which do not advance you or your proposition of generation of purpose and direction, will suck precious time away in an environment where you are likely to be judged on your six months' impacts and progress within the business.

Lack of direction and performance could also be a commentary on the maturity of your product or solution in the market. Pivots and changes of strategy are inevitable in business, especially early-stage ones, and also your big bets will not always come off. If the sales teams are left without clarity of where and how they can win in the market, you will find a disintegration of market or customer focus to one of chasing any clear and present opportunity. You will also find the focus of internal sales or wider company meetings are degenerating into the discussion of the reasons why you are not winning, not a focus on how and where you can win and what needs to be true in the future to promote future gains and growth. Consider in this the role of storytelling. Just as a great salesperson must be able to show how their solutions will provide value or efficiency to the customer, so must your team be able to clearly tell the stories of the customers and the market to your organization so that actionable intelligence leads the day.

> *Your challenges are not unique and you are not alone.*

Again, it is worth reiterating the point. It honestly does not matter what industry or level of experience you have, you will soon find that the challenges you face are universal. It is important to allow yourself to recognize this.

I was recently asked to participate in a cross-regional gathering of young sales managers in South-East Asia. People were representing from all manner of industries: oil and gas, construction, software, cloud, payments, fintech, and retail. The young managers were diverse, representing both sexes and a multitude of cultures and countries including Singapore, Malaysia, Vietnam, Indonesia, and Thailand.

The group was asked as an exercise to identify and then discuss in breakout groups the top three challenges they currently faced as newly promoted managers. They were then asked to come back to the whole group and to present their findings. I was stuck by how universal the challenges were. I recognized many from my own experience in sales leadership as well.

Examples included how to create a team sensibility, how to promote people skills in the organization, how to help teams help themselves as opposed to constantly escalating issues, how to coach and develop an identified talent to take more responsibility and act like a leader, how to handle a blocker or difficult personality, how to bridge teams to counter dysfunctional silos, and how to create and communicate a strategy with buy-in from senior leaders.

The takeaway for me is that no matter what you are facing, you are never really alone. Yet, it is easy and forgivable to feel as if the challenges you have with an individual or the circumstances within your company are utterly unique to you and you alone. It is still to this day in business a received wisdom that it is "lonely at the top," which, if it is, is an entirely wrong approach to the challenge. If you think and act that way, you might indeed be one of the problems.

If you are lonely at the top, then you are doing something wrong.
—Taken from *Leadership Gold* by John Maxwell. Copyright
© 2008 by John C Maxwell. Used by permission of
HarperCollins Christian Publishing.
www.harpercollinschristian.com.

So, how to prevent yourself from being sucked into immediate issues, how to create an environment where all are pulling in the right direction, and how to not become isolated as a leader? Within the subsequent chapters, we will look at each of the following:

- Changing your mindset to approach new challenges.
- Easing the transition of no longer working as a single contributor.
- Managing your new relationships within the management team.
- Quickly spotting the priorities to focus on.
- Creating your 90-day plan.
- How to set a tone, a direction, or a strategy.
- Communication and sharing information to gain support and followership.
- Dealing with difficult people who may question why you are in the role and not them.
- Building a mission.
- Creating a performance culture.
- Pipeline metrics and management.
- Setting yourself up for success for the next financial year.
- Asking for support and investment.
- Sales plan alignment, monitoring, pivots, and pipeline management.
- Coaching and mentoring.
- Spotting and nurturing talent.
- Building a highly functioning team that does not escalate every decision to you.
- Looking forward and looking around corners—carving out time to focus on the three- to five-year perspective and not just your current financial year.
- What to do when things are not going well.

I will attempt to cover all of these aspects and I will also attempt to place them into various scenarios that you might face as a sales leader as your journey develops and grows.

A Lifelong Career in the Service of Others

Sales is a team sport. If you are reading this book, I would assume you are considering developing your sales leadership as the focal point of your career. Sales and sales leadership should be fun. If it is not, something is going very wrong somewhere and, do not forget, just because you are now the leader, you should and can never stop selling. In my experience, pipeline and metrics jockeys do not make great sales leaders. Those that are closest to their markets and customers do.

To create buy-in and followership, you will need to sell internally across your entire stakeholder base. To forge success, you will need to sell to your customers as the figure head of your commercial business. You will also need to sell your mission and workplace to your colleagues' current and future. You want to build a reputation for being the place to work in your sector. Becoming the figurehead for your unit, division, region, or business is how you will truly lead from the front.

We will explore in more detail exactly how to achieve this figurehead status and, as a by-product, create the winning culture that will propel you toward your goals and ambitions. You will make people better than when you found each other; you will create hard-working, safe, and fun environments; and you will show a keen interest in your people beyond your function and corporate life. In exchange, they will challenge you, but will also give you their trust in developing your plans and executing within your teams. You will build culture.

Takeaways

- *Remember, you are not alone and your challenges are not unique.*
- *Do not rush in headlong; gather your data points and consider the stage of sales leadership you are facing.*

CHAPTER 3

Scenarios You Will Face

Chapter Summary

- In this chapter, we will focus on the three main scenarios you will face as a sales leader within a career and how to focus, prioritize, and manage oneself in the early stages of these roles on the path to strategy and culture build.
- Managing yourself: we will focus on negative emotions and the stories we tell ourselves as well as how to change these narratives.

In the previous chapter, we established that there are various stages of sales leadership; now, let's put a name to them and specifically think about the challenges and pressures you will be facing, which will be unique to each of them. More critically, let's consider how you will start to make sense of what is most important in order to allow yourself the best chance for successful culture building.

The scenarios you will face in your sales career can be broadly summarized into three categories:

- Promotion
- Turnaround
- New build

I will refer to these examples throughout our journey as the challenges for the sales leaders are different in each case.

- *Promotion*
  - o When you are promoted from within an existing team. This is probably your first sales leadership appointment.

You've likely not asked for or received any focused training
to help you transition to the new role.

- *Turnaround*
  - o You are coming into an organization from outside and
    likely hired with full visibility that the team you are joining
    is not performing as per expectation or potential. This
    could be for a host of reasons. It could also be because the
    previous leader has moved on, requiring you to perform
    a reset. Quite possibly, the environment you are entering
    is toxic or, at the very least, morale could be low and the
    team may be susceptible to flight risks. It is not unusual
    for the promotion scenario to have led ultimately to the
    turnaround scenario you have been brought in to address.
- *New build*
  - o The blank slate—from hire number one to strategy
    development and building your winning team. In this
    scenario, you could also be a player coach until you have
    built out the market strategy and your team to address the
    opportunities you have defined for your product or service
    in the market. You also have your pick from the talent in
    the market as you build out. It is likely that your priorities
    are about revenue now and hence you will need hunters
    able to deal with potentially more nebulous environments.
    These self-starter attributes will be key.

Promotion

You got the job! Well done, now you are likely wondering where to start
and how to do this. You are also most likely facing a whole new set of
challenges as your world will have shifted quite considerably. What is
your starting point?

Chances are you are already halfway or deep into the current financial
year. Consider where you are at. It is likely you are being faced with some
pressure on numbers but also consider that this is something of a free hit.
Do be conscious of the temptation to simply launch yourself at the role
without considering what has changed for you. Consider that this is an
opportunity to make significant changes and improvements. Launching

in headlong, most likely means that you will be ultimately maintaining the status quo under a different name, the danger being that you make no substantive impact on changing the course of direction for the better.

First, recognize that you will have a honeymoon period of goodwill toward you and your appointment, especially as you are an internal hire. You are probably inheriting someone else's plan, or it could well be that there is no plan at all other than a focus on the budget that has been set at the beginning of the year. This also means you have time to consider your role and where you have to focus before concentrating on the development of your next financial year's budget and plan.

You are stepping up to lead an established team—one you were not so long ago a member of. Some colleagues may be wary of you and, in some cases, possibly resentful that you have the role when they might think it should have been theirs. While all of this may be true, reflect that you are also known and have knowledge of the group. You are likely to need to build trust and followership anew. You will have existing relationships, backers, and supporters as well as those you need to win over. Start to consider what that makeup looks like and start also to think about those key relationships you need elsewhere in the organizational structure. Remember that you need to also build your relationships across senior leadership and across other functional areas that relate to your role.

Just because things are different does not mean that you are alone. Do be conscious of any emotion and especially any negativity that you may be feeling. This could be nervousness, imposter syndrome, or concern about potential conflict. This is all entirely natural, but taking these negative emotions into your new role is likely to make you view every moment through the lens of these. Start to isolate and address all of these emotions or feelings early. Try to identify and discern the reasons why you are feeling what you are feeling. You will need to be cognizant of these new inputs and the effects they may have in a way you never had to consider before. Ignoring and pushing on is not a recipe for helping to grow your leadership capability.

Negative Emotions

This aspect of being newly hired is worth double clicking on for a moment. We can all be our own worst critics, so check on your confidence levels and especially how unkind you are being to yourself. Remember, the stories we tell ourselves are a way of programming the mind.

Sometimes, we need to reprogram ourselves to break engrained, embedded neutral pathways and ways of thinking. So, start with your values and understanding what got you here. An exercise to help you to identify your values and abilities as part of defining your leadership brand is presented later in the book. Once you have done this, focus on your vision, mission, and goals and start to lean into some positive, more confident thoughts.

This can be challenging, especially if your industry is complex and you are unsure of where to start in your new role. This desire to get going can push inner reflection aside all too easily. The tools and templates presented later will provide a structured way for you to make sense of your business' data, so that you can identify priorities and undertake these tasks. It is, however, entirely on you to focus on managing yourself on your journey and to carve out the precious time to build the inputs that you can shape into a confident narrative to back yourself.

It is worth reiterating this. Carving out time for yourself is to acknowledge that you and what you are feeling is important and is a vital component in building a growth and success-driven culture. Remember that gathered data points on the business will highlight where you should put your focuses and will provide confidence through building a vision of how to proceed. Consider that your currently experienced emotions are just another of these data sets to gather and explore.

Remember also that it is all too easy to suppress the negativity we are feeling and to simply get busy being busy. There will be competition for your time so ensure you are not pulled hither and thither. Do not obsess about what you do not know. Half the battle here is giving yourself the time and space to find the data and to derive what it is telling you. The temptation to get cracking on the job is deflection of possibly uncomfortable reflection. The very real danger here is that you do not acknowledge the challenges you are facing openly, and therefore do not find the solutions or help you need in order to underpin your success in role.

Embarking on personal and professional growth often involves deliberate placing of oneself into uncomfortable situations. This concept is rooted in the idea that stepping outside of one's comfort zone is fostering learning, resilience, and adaptability. Yes, investigating your emotions and fears might be uncomfortable, but consider them an opportunity to grow and enhance your leadership capability. When individuals purposefully expose themselves to challenges or unfamiliar territories, including internal reflection, they confront new perspectives, skills, and experiences that contribute to their overall development. Ultimately, the process of growing through discomfort is a deliberate and proactive approach to self-improvement. It's about recognizing that true growth often lies just beyond the boundaries of familiarity and complacency, encouraging individuals to embrace challenges as stepping stones toward becoming their best selves.

Changing Neural Pathways and Fixed Thinking

Changing ourselves can sometimes be the hardest thing to do but it is entirely possible, and being in situations beyond our comfort zone is actually something one should strongly embrace in order to challenge oneself, as it is now that you can truly learn and grow.

Doing this needs a concerted effort though, so do carve out some time for you to surface and unpack each of the emotions you are feeling. It is worth it, because once done, you will have begun the process of breaking any triggered thinking or feedback loops that can happen in the moment of dealing with a person or situation.

Start by taking a moment to acknowledge the feelings you are experiencing and ask yourself in each case why they are there. Jot these down without immediately trying to find solutions; do not ignore them and do consider putting them through a positive forward-thinking structured exercise. An example framework exercise to undertake at this point would be to ask yourself some open questions:

- What am I feeling? (Lack of confidence, concern about what I do not know, imposter syndrome, not knowing where to focus, fear of conflict, etc.)
- What is the impact this emotion is having on me right now?

(Continued)

(*Continued*)

- Why am I feeling this way toward this situation or person or perceived weakness?
- What is the leadership shift I would like to make right now and why?
- How will I address these feelings the next time they arise?
- What is the one thing I could change to improve my performance?

By thinking about and answering these questions you are already putting anything negative you are feeling into a more positive light. Try to come up with a mission statement for yourself in response to this question. An example might be:

I want to be better at navigating complexity and change. I want to use effective and clear communication, while working collaboratively and in comfort with conflict.

This is a real example from my past. In order to create this, I was thinking about my position and the challenges I was facing real time at work in that moment. I was also at the time struggling with a key relationship with one of my colleagues. Your statement, therefore, should be honestly reflective of your own situation at any given time.

With a powerful mission or problem statement prepared, you can then review the journey you will need to make. This in turn can psychologically prepare you for the effort you will want to make to get to your destination. This is all in the context of you defining what it is you need to be in order to be able to win.

It is at this point that you can break down the components of the changes or actions you need to make into clear categories of where you are and where you would like to be. Examples could be mindset, behaviors, impact, and desired results. In terms of actions, these could be, for example, ask for training, ask for help, learn about a topic or a detail of your business or service, sit down and explore your working relationship with someone, or perhaps, openly discuss a restructure and how best to inform individuals or the team. Write these down somewhere and return to them as you evolve in your journey. Now, you can address those demons you have originally acknowledged and focus to work on thinking about the changes you will affect as you enter into your new role.

What is the leadership shift I would like to make right now?		
Answer: *(Clear, concise, truthful to yourself in the current moment, reflective of emotional state and concerns)*		
Element	From (Current)	To (Future)
Mindset		
Behaviors		
Impact		
Desired outcomes and results		
List: *(Clear, measurable, time orientated)* 1.		

Figure 3.1 Leadership shift template

Figure 3.1 is a template that you can use to capture elements you are keen to isolate and unpack. You could also add sections, for example, fears and negative emotions. The more precisely you define these, the more constructive your investigation into them can be.

This is of course an exercise you can do at any stage of your career so keep it in your locker to take out and help you through future challenges and situations as you develop your leadership style and approaches.

Leadership Is Learnt

Another reason why people are elevated to leadership roles without training is the suggestion that leaders are born. In fact, the reverse is true. The idea that leadership can be learned and developed through education, training, and experience is supported by numerous studies. This is a great reason to ask for help and training early in your appointment. Some influential research and theories in this field include:

- Warren Bennis and Burt Nanus, in their book *Leaders: Strategies for Taking Charge* published in 1985, argue that leadership is not a fixed trait but can be developed through self-awareness, experience, and learning.

- James MacGregor Burns introduced the concept of "transformational leadership," the idea that leadership could inspire and motivate teams to achieve more than they thought possible.
- Carol Dweck's work on the "growth mindset" has implications for leadership development. Having a growth mindset means that you believe you can develop your abilities and approaches through effort and learning

Be confident then that you are also on a journey and make it a discipline to embrace continuous learning and development of yourself.

A Changed Relationship

We will discuss the sales team in more detail later in the book, but do acknowledge that you will now have a new and different relationship with the team you are a part of. You will need to assess the team in a different light and by a different set of criteria. Be prepared for this and acknowledge that the dynamics have changed. Be honest and transparent. You should think about structuring one-to-one time with each team member in the group as well, for what has changed for you has also changed for them.

You may also feel under pressure to have answers or plans immediately, which is unreasonable. Remember, people may feel unnerved by the changes and will want to know what you and the leadership are thinking. You may not have these answers defined in anyway right now to be able to clearly communicate, so take your time to build your plan and communication approach. Do not be afraid to ask for that time and patience from others. The worst thing you can do right now is to jump into driving business as usual. This may feel tempting, but the risk here is that you may observe and change nothing other than the energy and perspective you throw into the role.

Do be open and approachable to addressing any concerns people may have. This will demonstrate values of openness and vulnerability. Now is the time to begin to collate the material that will allow you to present your strategic summary of where you want to take the business. Data is your friend in this respect and now you have to acknowledge that you need to also view the business differently than you did in the past.

Why Does This Scenario Occur as Much as It Does?

Hiring from within is often something that happens within sales teams, often for good reasons but also for reasons of immediacy, timing, and budget.

First and foremost, developing and growing your existing talent into leadership positions is a great thing for businesses. You keep all the gained experience and intellectual IP of the person, thus saving time and money on onboarding, as well as the inevitable time it takes for someone new to learn a new environment and sometimes a brand new industry.

It can also be good for the wider morale, as it can show faith and reward to the person being uplifted, as well as showing the rest of the team that the potential for advancement also exists. Then there is the hope element: the hope that by promoting someone already successful in their own right, might also confer this success onto the rest of the team and therefore uplift all-round performance.

As discussed earlier, this is not always a clear shot to success. Often, this fresh appointment can lead again to a change of the guard within a short period of time, perhaps within a year or two, should the results not manifest as desired. It would then be that the company in question starts to look for the more experienced (and usually more expensive) outside appointment, who has the capability to perform a total reset of the organization and the strategy to get there.

Turnaround

When entering the turnaround situation, you are most likely entering a brand new company, so you will have a lot to absorb. You might even be entering a brand new industry as I have done on a number of occasions, which enormously increases the learning curve ahead of you. One of the keys to getting a head start will be maximizing your learnings in the interview process.

You will have picked up a number of pointers no doubt throughout the interview process, but remember, you are looking from the outside in and you will need to test these assumptions as part of learning your new company. Make sure you do this on the way in so that you might gain invaluable feedback on where you think the priorities and challenges lie.

These days it is usual to go through a number of discussions within an interview process to join a company. Sometimes, these panel interviews can be quite wide ranging, affording you a chance to ask questions of various executives in the company. In this sense, you are interviewing the company as much as they are interviewing you.

Every discussion brings you the chance to ask questions and test assumptions as much as it is the time to show your qualities and approach to the role on offer. Already within this process, you should be able to identify the allies who will be able to help you, steer you, and corroborate what you are learning. You do not have to be 100 percent accurate at this point, and a solid approach here will help you to be coached toward the right emphases on topics once onboarded.

We will focus on the data points you should build up in order to create your vision, plan, and ultimately your sales plan, but it is already likely that you have elements you can build on. These quite likely include a one pager outlining your proposed focuses and deliverables or perhaps even a full 90-day plan. You will, of course, have to continue to gather more inputs and test any assumptions you have made looking in from the outside, but now you can assess and analyze the realities you find on the ground.

Use the 90-day plan or even the cornerstone templates covered later in the book, to deliver your insights and approach to the interview panel. These will help to give you a structure to the process of corroborating what you have learnt on your journey into the company. They should also allow you to show something of yourself, your principles, your process, and help to differentiate you as well.

Remember, data and information are important to develop focuses and remove emotion. When you have a clear path, you will find that negative emotion will disappear. Do be conscious that not everyone will accept or like change, so prepare your communications to be positive, clear, and precise.

Identifying a cohort across the business that will help you build is important and you should share your insights with them. For example; when rebuilding the culture and having identified established team members I would build around, I would always include them in the interview process for new team members. Once I had shortlisted someone, I would have the team spend time with them, focused on fit for the role and fit for the culture. They would know by now what we were building, but this for me was all about cultural fit. Product, approaches, methods, and skills can all be taught but attitude and cultural fit is everything. If the team bought into the candidate as much as I did, then I knew the group would gel, support, and help shape the person coming in.

This is, of course, easier in a smaller group but, even then, I would ensure the team members screening the candidate were also from across our entire customer-facing team. Hence, a new sales person would be screened by sales, relationship management, customer service, and implementation. This really fostered a group ethic and enabled new starters to join with impact, as they already felt accepted and part of the unit if offered the role.

I have worked in organizations where hiring would be a lot more scatter logical. One example was where the Managing Director, (MD) would frequently directly hire people for functions without the functional leader's clear knowledge until the deed was about done! Often, this would lead to more questions than answers and a difficult onboarding for the new joiners. Trust and solidarity as well as sustained culture build were not at all at play in this approach. It would also exacerbate confusing reporting lines.

Managing Yourself Within A Growth Mentality

If embarking on a turnaround role, you are likely to be more experienced with at least two or three commercial leadership appointments under your belt. No matter how experienced though, you must still listen to yourself and manage any emotions or negative feelings that might be surfacing. I would say this is especially true if you are entering a brand new industry or an adjacent or fresh element of an industry's ecosystem. Refer to the previous sections under "Changing Neural Pathways and Fixed Thinking" for suggestions and a template to help you isolate and interrogate any negative feelings you may be experiencing.

At this stage of your career, you are most likely embracing a growth mindset toward tackling challenges and obstacles through seeing them as opportunities for growth. As popularized by psychologist Carol Dweck in her book *"Mindset: The New Psychology of Success,"* Dweck characterized a growth mindset as a belief that one's abilities and intelligence can be developed and improved through effort, learning and perseverance.

Key to a growth mindset is the belief that abilities and skills are not fixed traits, but can be developed and expanded over time. Failure and negative emotions are a part of the learning process. In contrast to a growth mindset, a fixed mindset is characterized by the belief that abilities and skills are fixed and that people cannot significantly change.

Even if you are struggling to fully embrace a growth mindset, using the technique outlined under "Negative Emotions," can help you to shift your predominant mindset and cultivate a more progressive approach. This is achieved through consciously addressing the emotions and feelings you are experiencing and interrogating them in a more positive way to identify solutions or actions. All it takes is conscious effort and practice, while finding the time to acknowledge and unpack each emotion.

New Build

Here, you are able to set the agenda completely. Quite possibly, you are already in the company as a single contributor or player coach. You might have spent some time getting to know the total addressable market (TAM) for your solutions. Likely, you have identified your use cases, the sectors, and clients you wish to hunt in. Hopefully, you have landed your hero client or developed a pipeline accordingly.

With anything new, even if your start-up has a name and reputation, you will have to sell to, as much as judge the talent you are assessing for selection. Having your cornerstone vision (which we will look into in detail later,) will help you to sell the vision and culture you are establishing. The beauty is you will be able to shape your hiring process toward looking for the qualities you need and the shared values and philosophies that will go into those approaches.

Finding Your Data Points—CRM and Non-CRM

Whatever stage you find yourself in, having managed yourself, finding and interpreting the data that tells the stories of your business is now a vital step for you to undertake. For a start, data is critical in sales leadership. You simply cannot function without it. Second, it is a vital step in helping to settle yourself. If you are experiencing any negative emotions, a data-driven pathway to action can be a powerful tool to mitigate anything holding you back, such as imposter syndrome, by providing you with clear, tangible priority actions.

Data will also form the ingredients of your strategy and go-to market plan. In order to assess your priorities and where you will focus, you will need a plan. This is especially true of effecting change or in building your culture. For this, you will need data points to both inform the plan and show you where the priorities lie. Data, or rather inputs that help to shape your focus priorities, also come in numerous forms. We will spend some time on customer relationship management (CRM) inputs later on, but for now we will focus on some of the impressions and wider inputs available to you as the sales leader.

What we are looking to achieve here is an initial set of inputs from which you can assemble your storyline for the business. We will now begin to focus on some of the stepping stones on the pathway to developing your plan for the sales organization—the tools which will enable you to build consensus and culture. We will break this journey down into portions, so as best to surface the critical areas for focus and action. Think of this as a layering series of exercises to enable you to think about the role in terms of yourself, your business, your priorities, your focus, and your plan. Each layer will help to build your understanding and will in turn still your mind, so that you can focus on communication and execution.

Data Point Layers

1. The enhanced strengths, weaknesses, opportunities and threats, (SWOT) analysis
2. The 90-day plan
3. CRM inputs

4. Your cornerstone plan—culture fused to sales strategy

5. The detailed sales plan

6. Deeper focuses, adaptations, and pivots

Takeaways

- *Always consider what your starting point is.*
- *Listen to yourself. Capture your instinctual feelings toward the challenge ahead of you.*
- *Do not just focus on the negative. What are the major opportunities and wins ahead?*
- *Ask: What is not in place and what needs to be done for you to be successful?*
- *Surface the priorities, threats, and asks, which will inform your cornerstone statement.*

CHAPTER 4

Enhanced SWOT Analysis

Chapter Summary

- In this chapter, we will begin the layering process that will begin to provide your fact base for considering where you need to set your strategic plans, and priorities for the business.
- Layer one will be to undertake an enhanced SWOT analysis.

Distracted by emotions? Feeling imposter syndrome? Unsure where to start or where to focus? A great first step would be to give yourself a moment to think, preferably away from the office, and to capture your immediate impressions and emotions on a range of topics to do with the business.

This is about giving you a moment to elevate yourself from the day-to-day work, allowing you to surface the key data points which will help you quieten the noise and allow you to focus on an action-based set of principles and planning. Not only will this give you confidence, but it will ensure that you are on the pathway to building your agenda, focuses, people, and go-to market plans. Gathering data which you can interpret and build a fact base around is the critical first step.

The fastest way to begin the journey into data gathering and insight, is to begin with a snapshot view of your perceptions of the business as you see them in the moment right now. The way I would propose to do this is through an adapted and enhanced SWOT analysis. A SWOT analysis is always a useful exercise. Just because it is ubiquitous, do not forget the power of this simple device. It does not have to take a lot of time either to accomplish a meaningful SWOT analysis on your business.

Brevity is often best and I would suggest you approach this exercise as you would a brainstorm, by capturing the elements that rise up and resonate to you in the moment. Jot them down immediately without analysis or trying to solve for them. You are looking for a gut reaction and a response to the business in which you find yourself, because immediate impressions count. You can reflect on these and think of the solutions later.

The Enhanced SWOT—Taking It a Step Higher

The basic exercise of surfacing the strengths, weaknesses, opportunities, and risks of your business will already be providing some food for thought. Consider a number of questions and perspectives to further develop your

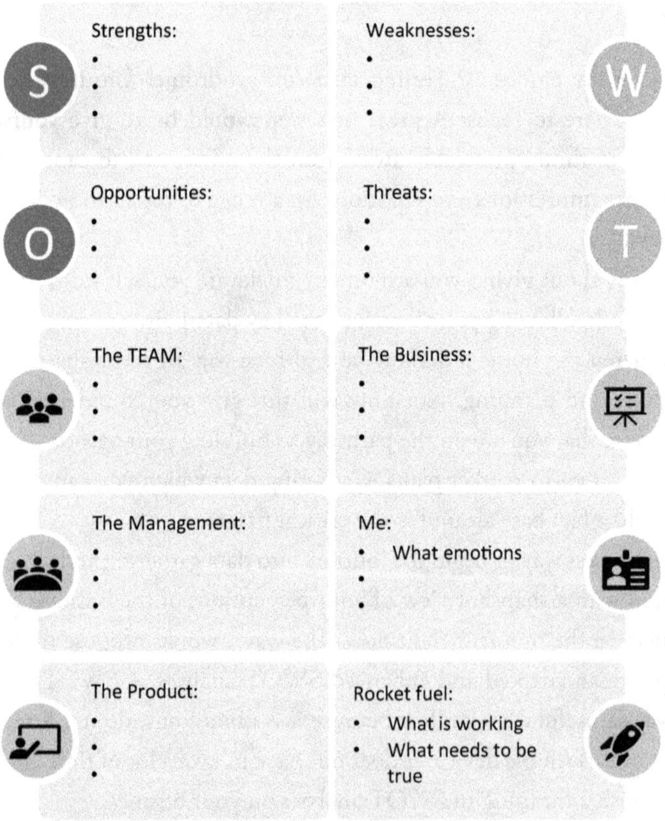

Figure 4.1 Enhanced SWOT

initial SWOT analysis. We do this because the basic SWOT will likely have pulled back a number of general issues across all elements of the business and we want to develop that more holistically in the context of your role. To go deeper, consider the template in Figure 4.1 and capture again the high-level themes to do with:

- The Team
- The Business
- The Management
- Me
- The Product
- The Rocket fuel—or what needs to be true to win?

Team

Broaden the exercise out to consider the people in your immediate team. One of your initial tasks in role will be to begin to understand these folks and their motivations, including their style of executing their business intimately.

Important within this are considerations of current performance, morale, and preparedness or ability to do their jobs to the best of their capacity. Include a GAP analysis of what skills, strengths, or approaches you feel are there or potentially missing. Does there need to be an accompanying hiring or training plan, for example, and if so, what do those plans look like? Questions you might want to ask yourself in collating your initial insights on the team could be:

- Who is who in your team?
- How are the internal team dynamics?
- Is there a good diversity of experience and approach?
- What is the atmosphere like?
- Who are the personalities and how do they interact across the group?
- Where is the team collectively and individually with respect to their targets?

(Continued)

(Continued)

- What came before? Are there legacy or past associations, for example, remaining loyalty toward the previous leader? Be specific and ask why there is a hangover, if indeed there is one.
- Does everyone know the collective mission and ultimate destination?
- Can each member of the team clearly articulate the mission and focus of the business right now?
- Are the KPIs, targets, commission structures, and market segmentations clear and understood by all?
- Who in the team is winning in the market and why? Who is struggling or needs support?
- Is there unity and sense of purpose? Or are there individualistic behaviors?
- Are there any skill gaps in the team?
- How is the team finding and converting its business?
- How is the team structured to find and win this business? Is it by industry, geography, customer size, or product? Is that working?
- Is business being left on the table? Is there a case for additional resource or market/product focuses?
- Are there cross-selling opportunities?
- Is there a clearly defined handover process from sales (new business) to relationship management or key account sales?
- Is there a new business plan and is there an existing customer or key account plan?
- How are major accounts being managed, is there a plan to grow, and how developed are these plans?
- Are relationship management (RMs) or key accounts functions treated as sales functions?
- Do RMs and key accounts carry quota targets?
- Do you see bowtie or diamond approaches to key account management?

- Are plans regional or global when unlocking strategic key account opportunity? Does your company act locally or globally? Or both?
- How are other functions such as finance, marketing, product, support, and implementation acting and reacting with the team?
- What is marketing's focus and how is it contributing to opportunity identification?
- How is product supporting the team to address opportunity in the market?
- Are standard solutions being sold or is there high customization each time, why is that, and what are the impacts?
- Is knowledge and expertise in the organization easily accessible and shared?
- Do we need to hire? What hiring plan exists? What skills are needed and where would we like to see candidates from?
- Is there a talent acquisition (TA) role or do we work with outside recruiters?
- What does the on boarding and training plan look like?
- What are the KPIs and targets the new joiner will take on?
- Is there a sense of culture within the organization and are there identified behaviors that are expected and aligned to meeting the company's financial targets and outcomes?
- Within the KPIs, are there "soft" targets in place to ensure cross-functional and collaborative behaviors are in focus?
- What is the annual review, individual target setting, and ongoing cadence like?
- Is 360 degree or step feedback sought and reviewed as part of a review process?
- How open and accessible is leadership?

In my experience, clarity of role, of where salespeople can hunt for opportunity, and how they get paid are critical. Any confusion can lead to dysfunction, bad morale, and flight risks. Ask yourself if the current structure and go-to market organization is serving your people. Are they distracted or focused? Identifying elements that might be holding your people back could enable you to deliver some quick wins aligned to your people-first principles.

Management

Management will have hired you for a reason and you should have a sense of what they are hoping to achieve in your appointment. Formally capture these elements as well, but also throw the net wider to consider how management is showing up in the business. How well is critical information shared and what support is management providing to help the commercial function win in the marketplace.

Questions you might ask could be:

* Why do you think management promoted you?
* Are you clear on their priorities and ambitions?
* Do you know who is who, who is supporting you, and where you can get support and advice if needs be?
* Where is the current business plan and what are the numbers in the current or next year's plan?
* When does the annual budgeting planning start and what is the usual process? Is it top down or is there alignment with commercial functions?
* How is the team measuring up against those numbers in the current period or at the point of your joining?
* What does the business expect of you? Do you align with what the management is saying to you about (i) people, (ii) performance, (iii) product, and (iv) go-to market strategy?
* Who will you need to bring on the journey when you have developed your plan?
* What investments will you need and how will you justify these?
* What is the dominant style and values of the leadership and how are those being experienced in the organization?

- What does success look like in six months to a year?
- How much access are you getting to leadership and what challenges do you see aligning your plans and approach to executive and cross-functional colleagues?

Ensuring that you have good access to, as well as clear communication and alignment with, your executive leadership function is critical to being able to share, develop, and execute your plan. You will need investment, support, and, at times, aircover to make the changes you need to win for the business. Time spent reviewing your current relationship with management, alongside what you would like that relationship to look like in six months to a year from now, is time well spent early on.

Me

Do not neglect yourself in this process. It can be easy to think you are acknowledging how you are feeling without taking the time to isolate and unpack these feelings. Battling issues on a day-to-day basis is not finding ways to understand what you are feeling and how to solve for these potential inhibitors to your being your best self. As such, do not progress without a check in, as this in itself will likely uncover critical insights as to where your concerns and current preparedness is in the moment. In terms of taking on the challenges ahead, ask yourself:

- How are you feeling right now?
- What are the specific emotions: confidence, nervousness, excitement, or fear?
- Why do you suppose you are feeling these specific feelings?
- Do you feel supported?
- Do you feel that you are more conscious of what you don't know as opposed to what you know you are good at?
- Is your role and are your targets well defined?

(Continued)

(*Continued*)

- Do you feel these are reasonable and sustainable in the market?
- What qualities have you been demonstrating that got you the role?
- What do you need to be successful?
- What are the top three priorities you need to focus on right now?
- What will success look like for you in 6 to 12 months?
- What leadership shifts are you conscious on needing to develop or enhance?
- What budgets do you have?
- Are there quick wins/low-hanging fruit?
- Where are you going to focus for the greatest outcomes?
- What are the must-wins? Do you have any transformative whale business to hunt down?

Combine this exercise with the technique in the earlier section "Negative Emotions" if you need to explore any emotion or feeling more deeply.

Product

If you are promoted from within the company having been a salesperson and possibly still carrying sales targets, you should already have a clear perspective on the product and how it is being received in the market. If you are joining a company, you will need to investigate with your team to build a perspective of how the product is currently being received and whether there are any enhancements or new features required. Questions you can ask yourself might be:

- Are there any glaring gaps?
- Where does your competition sit in product terms?
- How are customer and market feedbacks communicated?
- Is the sales function contributing to business case investment build in product development?

- Does the customer relationship management (CRM,) capture lost deals and can you put a number on deal opportunity lost to feature gaps?
- Is there a rigor to collating opportunity data to develop business cases for prioritized action?
- Where is the product roadmap and how is it shared?
- How does prioritization occur?
- How often does product present to the sales group and do they participate in customer, strategy sessions, and sales reviews?
- What are the new markets or features that you need to launch to propel the next phase of growth for the company?
- Are customers asked or are there client forums to gain their inputs on features or improvements they would like to see in terms of your product?

If you do discover that there are product gaps and that there is lost opportunity in the market, then you must build a recognition in the sales team that they have a responsibility to collate this data to help prioritization and business casing of new developments. Clear communication and close cooperation between the commercial teams and product is supremely important in this regard.

The Business

The next step is to consider the business itself. Taking this view is to helicopter up a level and, in so doing, you may well uncover aspects you have missed or did not previously consider in your thinking up to this point. Questions might be:

- At a high level, where do you think the business is right now on its journey, in the market, and in terms of its goals?
- Is the leadership engaged and visible?

(Continued)

(*Continued*)

- How is the company messaging its progress and updates?
- Is the business organized effectively to address the market—this could be reporting lines, new and existing sales mix (are they split or under one function?)
- Are all functions aligned in terms of goals?
- How well is the current commercial plan articulated, shared, and iterated?
- Is the company addressing its market well?
- Is the company known for its solution in the market? Is it the go-to, a disruptor, or an unknown name?
- Does marketing help with thought leadership and name recognition in the market?
- Where does the product sit in addressing and helping you to achieve the numbers?
- What does the product roadmap give you and by when?
- How is that feedback shared and prioritized?
- Is knowledge shared across functions or is it siloed?
- What are the key metrics you are being asked to deliver and how are they broken down?
- What are the baselines from which you are taking over against budget and any other key metrics set at the beginning of the year?
- What is the CRM system and how is it being used?
- How are numbers being reported now? Can you easily forecast your sales?
- How is revenue being tracked?
- Is there a buddy or mentorship plan in place?
- How is training asked for or budgeted?

By now, you will have gathered many inputs on the current state of the business and you are likely keen to begin to consider solutions for these. Before you do, quickly throw your mind into what might be called a "future-forward" mode. Ask yourself where you would like to see the business in three or five years' time. What could be the new fertile grounds for you to develop and sell into? What new markets or extended offerings could be created to address new untapped potential and what could these markets look like from a T-shirt-sized financial modeling perspective in dollar terms? I like to call this "rocket fuel."

Rocket Fuel

As a final step, change the lens from where the business is to where the business could be, and what it would take to get there. Try to elevate to a handful of big bets.

The SWOT takes into account surfacing of risks and opportunities but, as a sales leader, you now need to focus in on potential solutions matched against revenue potential. This is the first step toward creating a structured prioritization and potential business casing of investment.

I think of rocket fuel in the context of a three- to five-year plan. This might be an ask of product or the opening of a new market, which would unlock new potential to propel your business forward, but I think the idea is valid to think about from year one in role. Consider and identify areas where an investment could have a profound impact on the business. Another way to think about this is what are the two or three big bets you would make to create a transformative launchpad for the revenue profile. In order to start to think beyond the current moment, consider topics such as:

- Where do you currently play and win?
- Why are you losing and to whom?
- What are the expansion opportunities?
- Are there potentially new geographies to explore?
- What do you need to support your efforts to win?
- What needs to be true to win?
- Where does the product have holes compared to the competition or where could an enhancement or feature unlock potential?
- What is the financial impact this could have on the business?

Business Unit Spend and Net Profit

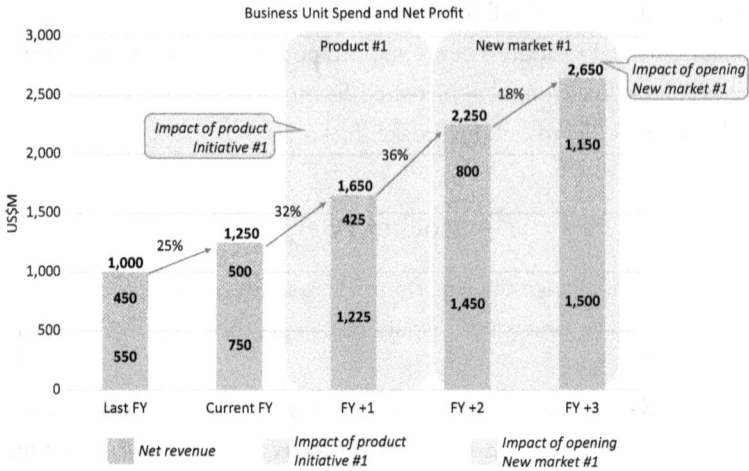

Figure 4.2 Rocket fuel financial step plan example—spend and net revenue

In terms of presenting what impact the rocket fuel could have on the business, I would show a financial step plan from current gross revenue and net revenue, to show the contributions of each new initiative to be able to present the three- to five-year journey in terms of potential financial growth. An example is shown in Figure 4.2.

More detail or structure could be added to break out the various contributors to growth, but this is a simple way to start to articulate your vision for the longer term trajectory.

Making Asks of the Business

This is an area that the newly promoted or junior sales leader will typically not consider. When new in role, the concept of asking for investment or help can be a difficult one as the individual's perspective is likely to be purely focused on the here and now of making an impact. They also might feel too nervous or out of their depth to make such suggestions.

As we have discussed, being purely immediacy focused on action and results is not at all likely to inspire or make lasting change. In my first sales leadership role, I remember feeling as if I could not ask for anything until I had proven myself and gained the buy-in of the management that had promoted me. I felt as if I had to return their faith in me tangibly, before I could ask for anything that might help or support me.

Looking back, this really makes no sense at all, but my head was very much in the trenches of the day-to-day business. Remember also, that any ask should be considered and backed by informed data and the vision you are setting out. You should also frame any asks in the context of the impact expected on the business. For you to develop more of a business case approach, you will again need to go through the layering steps suggested, to assemble your data points and surface what it is you need to focus on in order to affect the greatest impacts on your business in terms of hitting and exceeding target.

I would suggest that this is again not a process to rush. Ensure you have identified what needs to be true to win without jumping fully to the ask. This is also a question worth asking of your team as well as gathering the insights of your fellow functional leaders. Try always to bring a rounded view of what you are proposing to the business. Thinking of this as a sale also helps; your goal is to get to the buying questions, which will allow you to better build out your business case.

Building toward your overall strategy statement is also crucial in order to land the request on the business, but first do begin to gather data inputs which will help you make the case. The cornerstone template, which we will discuss later, will allow you to align this with your management. Do not forget that one of your asks could be that you are provided training to help adapt to your new role. Other asks could be for new hires, individual training, product investment, or tools to help you execute, such as CRM investments, marketing budgets, and events.

Be cognizant that you have been hired to lead the function and you are asking here to be supported in that task for maximum outcome. Think of it this way: the company has already backed you; they should also invest in you, your vision, and your success. Do have the materials ready for the deeper questions in terms of what will be the volume or revenue impact of the ask you are making and within what timeframe these results should be expected. If you are asking for training, come with the proposed courses, costings, and timings in hand, along with the impact justifications you are hoping to gain.

Make Asking What Do We Need to Win a Habit

In this chapter, we are clearly focusing on the first 30 days of your role. This is the period when you are getting your feet under the table of your new position. You are on receive, learning about the people and the business, while fitting all gathered data points toward the financial goals that have been set for your function.

Do not think that this is the end of the exercise. Managing a financial year is nothing if not a fluid business. You will need to review your set plan and see what is working and what is not. You will likely need to pivot. Each mature deal in your pipeline is an individual campaign you need to focus and finish on, by successfully signing and onboarding your new client to the business. Each identified key account will need its executive buying cohort mapped out, perhaps globally, and will need identified opportunities and plans attached to maximizing the full revenue opportunity, while also defending the customer against competition. It is therefore critical that you think in terms of what is needed for the team and plan to be successful at all times. You should always be gathering inputs from individuals and the team, making it a good habit to ask continuously, "is there anything I can do to help?" as well "what do we need to win here?"

By doing so, not only are you closely attuned to what is needed in each deal and across your business plan, but you are also conveying to your team and fellow leaders a sense of creatively thinking about your business in terms of overcoming challenges and opening up new opportunities. Velocity is the key in any sales engine; asking the question puts your people into the mindset of creatively focusing and finishing, always.

This is one of the critical cultural behaviors you want to instill early across your group and into cross-functional areas as well. By asking these questions of others and not prompting their responses, you are conveying to others the responsibility to think holistically about their, and the overall, business.

Takeaways

- *Take the time to capture the snapshot of the business as it presents to you at this time.*
- *Enhance the analysis to consider people (including yourself), the business, management, the product, and the rocket fuels that could catapult your growth.*
- *Consider what is needed to win—make this a habit.*
- *Begin the cultural shift of placing creative ownership on others in the business.*
- *Consider this step one of building your culture, direction, and plan.*

CHAPTER 5

Your 90-Day Plan

Chapter Summary

- The 90-day plan is the next layering process after your enhanced SWOT.
- If you are not already regularly using 90-day plans for interview and within your job, consider them as a means of differentiation, to manage your time and to help you focus on your key identified priorities.

Having spent some time with the enhanced SWOT, you will have at your fingertips a heap of insights and data points gathered, which represent a holistic view of the company. You will now naturally be shifting your focus into organizational matters and problem solving. A next step to build on the themes of the enhanced SWOT is to now drill into where you will focus your time initially and toward what objectives. Here, we think of the 90-day plan.

A 90-day plan serves a number of uses: first, in setting yourself some guardrails. You are putting your commitment and time toward certain key activities and outcomes and, next, by creating and sharing the plan, you are also holding yourself to be accountable to timelines and deliverables.

The window of opportunity in your first three to six months in a business is quite tight. One can easily get pulled in multiple directions which serve the short term and do not set you or your business up for success long term. A 90-day plan will help to focus your mind on what is most important, what can be ignored, and what help you will need to achieve identified quick wins, as you lay down the foundations for a more concerted build toward an executable plan.

Bear in mind you may already have a 90-day plan structure in place, especially if you are a new hire coming into a business. A 90-day plan is of course a great way to help to differentiate yourself in an interview process, as not only does it help to give yourself a template or structure for the initial days within the job, but it also provides your hiring panel with an insight into your philosophy and processes.

The 90-day plan lives long beyond your getting the job. It is a living tool that can be used multiple times and across your development in your career. It is the next step on identifying and shaping the data inputs from your business, allowing you to mold them into a narrative, a vision, and the focused mission beyond this. Think of this as a layering process. Again, as with the enhanced SWOT, this is all formulating the raw materials into a pattern that will help you to build your culture.

Promotion

From the perspective of the newly promoted, the 90-day plan can build on and develop the enhanced SWOT analysis you conducted initially. The enhanced SWOT will have identified a number of key themes. Now, you can start to put some emphasis, prioritization, and time-based intent on finding solutions, support, or pathways to change. Both are excellent ways for you to leverage all of your experience and knowledge of the business you have been in, and you will now serve from a new perspective.

Creating these documents again provides another golden opportunity to present to your leadership, test your assumptions and viewpoints, and align these topics and priorities with the wider management group. If you are going to be making asks of the business to support you, a communicated 90-day plan, aligned to your executive leaders, will go a long way toward helping you to achieve the buy-in you are asking for.

Turn Around and New Build

In these scenarios, you of course may already have a 90-day plan. If it is not yet fully formed, then at least have a one pager indicating something of your approach and something of what you intend to deliver and focus on, aligned to values and asks of the business, (we will investigate the values and behaviors element within the cornerstone chapter and beyond.) A one pager which could in time be developed into a 90-day plan could look like the example in Figure 5.1.

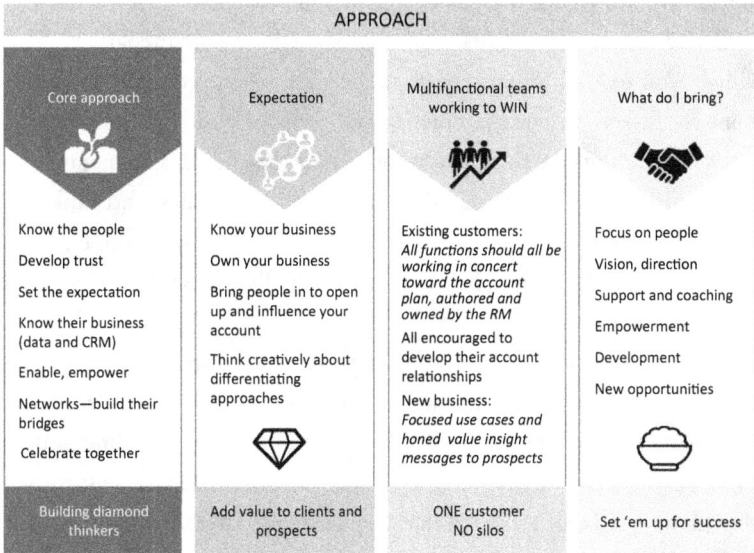

APPROACH			
Core approach	Expectation	Multifunctional teams working to WIN	What do I bring?
Know the people	Know your business	Existing customers:	Focus on people
Develop trust	Own your business	*All functions should all be working in concert toward the account plan, authored and owned by the RM*	Vision, direction
Set the expectation	Bring people in to open up and influence your account		Support and coaching
Know their business (data and CRM)		All encouraged to develop their account relationships	Empowerment
Enable, empower	Think creatively about differentiating approaches		Development
Networks—build their bridges		New business:	New opportunities
Celebrate together		*Focused use cases and honed value insight messages to prospects*	
Building diamond thinkers	Add value to clients and prospects	ONE customer NO silos	Set 'em up for success

Figure 5.1 How did I get here—how will I get there?

This one pager could best be described as an insight into "how did I get here and how will I get there." In summary, it outlines basic focuses and approaches that you might undertake when entering a business for the first time.

Using 90-Day Plans in Interview

If you are regularly interviewing without a 90-day plan or one pager, I would highly recommend that you work on and deliver these as part of your interview process, as these documents can often help to seal the deal for you. In fact, the cornerstone template is also easily adapted to be your interview one pager on proposed focuses and outcomes as a candidate. Bear in mind that the cornerstone is a more strategic document in nature. Be careful in what interviews you use the cornerstone, as you may want to focus on more basic executional sales management topics initially.

Using documents like these not only provides the hiring company with a structured approach which details something about your processes, philosophy, and personality, but also allows you to test out ideas and perceptions that you may have coming into a business. It allows you to craft a deeper conversation in interview as you will have raised up substantive, impactful topics and ideas for approaches.

There is a lot of research you can do in interview preparation that will get you to a 70/80 percent accuracy level, when preparing the document for interview. For example, you've got your basic due diligence on the web: reading the company website and the public statements such as annual reports, finding out about the published values, and LinkedIn research on the executives. Other websites such as glassdoor.com may also provide some cultural insights. Do not take it all at face value; always test your assumptions and broaden your data set.

Do consider, as well, actively using your network, asking connections or friends who may know the company you are interviewing for, or indeed the company executives themselves for additional time to pose questions and test the premises you are developing. You will be surprised how many will help, provided that you come prepared and make the ask in a compelling manner. I have turned down job opportunities based on this type of interview outside of the hiring process. You can never have enough insight and data when making a critical decision.

More than once in my career, using these documents has turned conversations into job offers. Both are also exercises in being comfortable with what you do not know, as you likely have only to work on perceptions and inputs gleaned throughout your conversations, research, and interview process to date.

Based upon my experience of interviewing folks for roles, I know and suspect that few people do this research with a view to providing a platform for deeper interview conversations. I suspect this is largely out of fear of being off the mark, but consider the benefits in terms of differentiation from other candidates and also developing fact-based conversations about the actions you would take in the business. It really is a springboard to an effective start to your time in role.

In fact, I am always unpleasantly surprised by the candidates' lack of research. So many times, in interview, the candidate will base insights on the company website alone, which can often be misinterpreted. Such "research" is never enough. I always prefer a candidate who has shown the initiative to dig deeper and present themselves in a differentiated manner than those who do nothing or just the bare minimum.

Be confident in the fact that you will not know all things at this stage, as someone looking into a business from the outside. If you can substantiate or test assumptions by reaching out to connections on LinkedIn, then so much the better, but 100 percent accuracy is really not the aim here. I think this is an important point to unpack some more. Remember, any document you prepare in the interview process does not have to be 100 percent accurate; it is about having a deeper conversation. After all, you are coming into an organization and you cannot possibly know all the data points and landscape looking in from the outside. Having made this effort, it is also more probable that the interviewer will help to coach you, allowing you to hone both the understanding and your proposed actions and focus areas, thereby strengthening your case for hire even further.

Do revisit the document when you arrive on deck. That is why taking the time to reassess when you do arrive is fundamentally important. The enhanced SWOT and 90-day plan give you the tools to maintain a living record.

The New Start

Here, you want to be focusing on a keen understanding of your value proposition in the market. Where do you want to target for the most impact and value? Depending on the maturity of your proposition, this is largely going to be driven by your overall business plan, existing markets, existing customers, and your ability to service and support geographically.

In this respect, you are likely to need to liaise with and align to a larger strategy or company vision, asking yourself what the geographies, segments, and customers are that you are addressing. Your plan is likely to be about focus, focus, and focus and not spreading yourself too wide and chasing after everything that might be out there.

A 90-Day Plan Template

Figure 5.2 is a template that you can use or adapt for the creation of your full 90-day plan. A 90-day plan is a document used to chart the first 30,

60, and 90 days within a new organization. For the sales leader, it is a template that can be used to:

- Help organize your thoughts and previously gathered impressions and data.
- Communicate something of one's methodology and approach.
- Help to create specific, actionable, and measurable plans tied to the role's mission.
- Help capture perceptions and expectations of the role in the early days.
- Help depressurize you and to bring clarity to the challenges ahead.
- Help lay out the actions that will surface the prime focuses and priorities, which will inform your cornerstone and ultimately your ongoing sales plan.

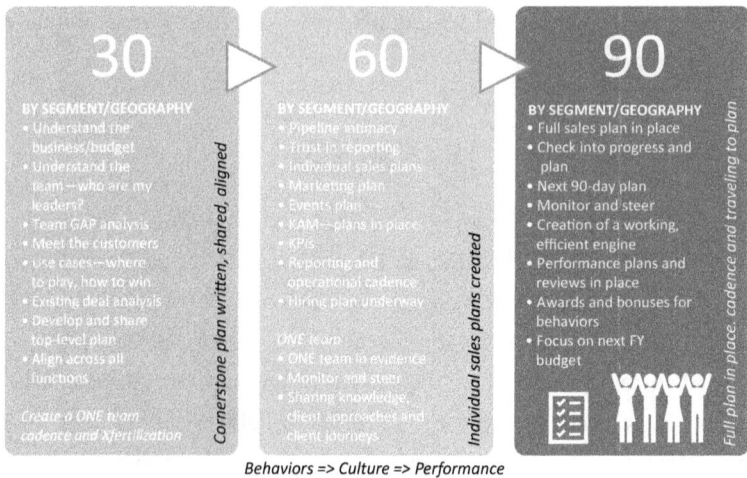

Behaviors => Culture => Performance

Figure 5.2 A 90-day plan template

It is important to keep the 90-day plan succinct, simple, and clear. Do not spell out the detail and keep it high level. Detail can be discussed in face-to-face sessions. It is important to revisit it, as well as use the resultant inputs and outcomes to help create your cornerstone strategy on which the rest of your sales plan can be assembled.

Takeaways

- *Your time is precious.*
- *You want to ensure that you maximize the time you are using to directly impact the business.*
- *Start to think about 90-day plans:*
  - *For interviews.*
  - *For ongoing self-cadence.*
- *Make the 90-day plan part of your managerial workout routine.*
- *Use to prioritize and manage your time.*
- *Communicate the plan, test the assumptions, and align across the business.*
- *A living document—review and make sure the plan is still relevant and that you are honoring it.*

CHAPTER 6

Getting to Know Your People

Chapter Summary

- Getting to know your people as individuals, the team dynamics, group morale, and capabilities requires availability, humility, vulnerability, curiosity, and authentic interest. It is a vital step toward identifying what is ahead of you in the task of building your behaviors and culture.
- Be prepared to manage difficult conversations, situations, and even hostility in the early days. Always gather your own impressions and insights and be receptive to wider causes of conflict or blockage within the organization.

No matter which scenario you are facing and as part of your essential data gathering, you need to know who is with you on the journey. You also need to assess what the scale of the task will be in terms of culture building and where the existing centers of leadership are that will help you to foster and grow this aligned community going forward.

In human relationships, trust is key and trust comes from aligned values and goals. Critically, however, trust also comes from creating an open and safe space, wherein people can feel heard and raise opinions without fear. This can be defined as creating the environment within which people can be their true selves and have an honest and transparent conversation with one another, including difficult conversations.

As a people-first leader, this requires you to offer availability, humility, and vulnerability. By showing something of yourself, your values, and your philosophy of commercial leadership, you will not only gather critical insights from others, but also begin the process of molding your team by creating followership. It also means being consistent in all interactions, whether one-to-one, group meetings, town halls, or socially.

What's the first step? Authentic leadership starts with curiosity and interest. Both work and nonwork bonding is a vital part of this. Ultimately, you want to know what makes your people tick, what are their motivations and their values, how do they think about and relate to the business, and how do they interact with others. By assessing where people are, you can formulate your plan of how to get to where you are going.

Reassessing the group dynamics is especially vital when you are either newly promoted or parachuted into a nonfunctioning environment. Take a minute to look at those around you and think about your appointment as if you were in their shoes. Think about how they are feeling and what questions they are probably asking themselves. What is the current mood and reaction of people to you? Be available for open exchanges of ideas and concerns; as stated before, do not be afraid to ask for time before you can fully convey the direction of travel. These initial discussions should be about discovery.

Not only are you looking to align and build, but you are also looking for the pillars of your new culture and values, those people that will in turn be your leaders, and who will embrace the new journey together with you. It is these people who will live the behaviors that will underpin and create your culture. Finding these heroes early is critical to building your team. By exemplifying the values and behaviors that will shape your culture, both you and your team will steer the mission forward. Do not be shy to tell these critical players that you are conferring on them this leadership role and bring them into decision making and people decisions where appropriate.

Let's think about the end state for a moment. What is it that we are ultimately looking for? To my mind, a functioning culture is where each team member is crystal clear on where they play, laser focused on how they win. They understand and are bonded to the mission and objectives set. They take responsibility for being expert in their markets, customer base, and the value proposition that you bring through your product or service. They feel recognized and heard. They have a learning or growth mentality and seek enhanced ways to solve for their customer's challenges and for how they best articulate that value. They have established and are operating internal networks and step relationships with senior management. They know how to source their own solutions and think creatively about how to overcome challenges and obstacles. They support one another and build bridges to win across your organization. They have fun and they also stand up for and reinforce the behaviors and culture that have been built as a matter of course. Escalations are raised once due diligence on considering solutions has been undertaken. There is full participation and trust across the group and the data and insights learned are shared and can be trusted.

Seems implausible or the unachievably perfect scenario? It is not, but it is a journey to get to this point. It is also something you cannot think of as a one-time deal. If you are not living the culture you want full time, then all the energy you have expended defining the values and behaviors you wish to see will be for naught. Nothing is worse than a management suite that has created a cultural document in isolation, published and celebrated it, only for that same management to assume that the job is done. This is the height of insincerity. You have to be prepared to invest your time and yourself completely to the project. It all takes time and needs to be jealously guarded once established, as culture is also the most fragile thing. What you want as the leader in a new hire or turnaround situation is to seek to achieve this end state, or see signs of it, within a year of your tenure or sooner.

Once you have this in place, you as the leader can focus on the job of getting out of your team's way through supporting them and can focus on the longer term and strategic enhancements to your direction. The true benefit to you once you have established a performance culture, is that you will then become freer to do the work of looking around corners and seeking the opportunities that can inform your three- to five-year plan. This, in and of itself, is also a critical step in binding people to your mission. All too often in sales, we only see the current year and targets ahead of us, which are only reset as we run again to face the challenges of the next year. When we have a sense of the horizon extending beyond this financial year and that we are building and contributing to a much larger mission, then there is a greater cultural binding opportunity and the rewards all round are elevated.

You will of course have to pivot tactically on occasion and seek new approaches. Things will not always go according to plan. Indeed, a pillar principle of a good plan is that the plan is likely to need to change or adapt at any given point. The difference with having a vibrant culture alongside you is that you will have with you an engaged cohort of people, who are also creatively thinking about their individual businesses, as well as the overall enterprise, and will be doing so in an aligned manner. This makes the task of pivoting or seeking new ideas or approaches easier to navigate.

Take it one step at a time. The initial step in building your team is to evaluate the current state, identify needs, and determine the leaders around whom you will construct it. Once you have built it, be conscious of how fragile it is and how much you will need to consistently focus in order to maintain your performance culture. Lay down behaviors by demonstrating them yourself. Jealously protect and always have an eye out for your culture. It can be easy to get complacent; ensure the fires are burning and that your people are motivated to strive and win for you. Remember, it all takes time and that it is a layering process.

The Promotion

This can be a real challenge for the recently promoted manager or sales leader. Suddenly, everything has changed. Before, you were a part of the collective; now, you are a leader and you may suddenly find that leadership is a lonely business. In truth, it is not, unless you choose it to be, but it is easy to feel isolated.

Be prepared for some team members to treat you differently, even with suspicion, nervousness, or sometimes resentment. Your friends in the team will likely remain your friends but even then, things have altered subtly as you are now the boss and there will come a time when you may have to focus on business as opposed to your relationship. You must also be conscious of favoritism, either real or imagined in terms of the time you spend with people and the emphasis perceived.

Be open to having a vulnerable conversation across the group. Your privileged position of being promoted from within the unit will not convey onto you continued insider insight, unless you can build trust.

Be cautious of trying to fully set out your stall or agenda too early. If you launch into addressing what you see as priorities, without embracing the individuals, you could easily find yourself truly isolated through coming off as detached or, worse still, arrogant. Ask for the time to learn.

Be cautious of the directions your leadership might be encouraging you to take, until you have firmed up your inputs and you are ready to make your own decisions, especially around people. Multiple times in my career, when promoted to manage people, I was told that I would likely have to fire one or more of the individuals within the team. On a few occasions, these were actually people in their first ever sales roles. The managing directors in these cases had already made their minds up and believed the people in question were going nowhere. In each case, these leaders were only using or observing one data point, as the individuals in question had been utterly neglected. Present performance is not always the complete story. One data point without engagement can lead to false conclusions being made.

I have always opted to formulate my own judgments. With one individual, I took him for a drive and we had a lunch away from the office. Over the course of this meal, I discovered that our so-called nonperformer had really not been set up for success at all. He had been offered no training or attention and was caught between his manager (who was something of a single contributor in the worst sense) and the managing director. Both had neglected this person.

In getting to know this individual and his personal drivers, I recognized someone frustrated by the lack of support he had been given; critically, I also saw ambition and a desire to learn. He understood the opportunity, wanted to be a success at the company, and was passionate about the business. This was actually a talent that needed nurturing, support, and guidance. Not only did this person become a valued member of that company and a dear friend, but today he has a senior management role within the sales leadership of one of the world's largest global IT firms. Take your own time to assess the talent on deck and the motivations of your people.

Sometimes, it's more of an adjustment of attitude, matched to some key, meaningful, measurable, and time-bound KPIs, that is required to turn around a performance. In these instances, it's usually a frank or sometimes difficult conversation which is needed to ascertain if the motivation is there and whether the opportunity is fully understood, assuming there are no other issues at play. If this is the case, listening, finding out what is happening, and providing support could be the key.

By way of illustrating this, another experience I had was of a salesperson who was exhibiting aggressive and noncollaborative behaviors toward other employees. Sometimes, this could also be witnessed in certain customer interactions. The person in question was the most successful in quota terms and the most experienced in the group. The issue was that he was effectively rough-roading other functions to service his clients as a priority. This was being delivered in a highly dismissive way, which ensured he was losing the support of others.

In these instances, you have to be able to have an honest and difficult conversation with someone. Always start by stating that you must convey some difficult points and ask to proceed. This should help to defuse any defensiveness there may be, if you were to otherwise jump straight into the topic. What you do not want to do is create a confrontation, but instead, gain some acknowledgment that things are unsustainable in their current form and that an agreed path must be taken to reconcile and improve matters.

Another colleague I worked with in one of my teams was seen to be underperforming and grumpy toward the group, I took time to analyze the data and observed data points which included some unfortunate engagements with others on the team. He was effectively alienating those around him, who would avoid or not seek to support him, which only made matters worse.

Once I had established that this person was indeed motivated to succeed and was intent to work hard to improve, it was a matter of clearly setting the behaviors required to be successful, which included working on improving their internal team dynamics. We set soft KPIs on these points. It so happened that this person was dealing with some highly challenging personal issues and stresses, that he was taking out on others, as he did not know how to ask for help. Not so long after our conversations and subsequent goal setting, I had the enormous pleasure to present this person with an achievement award; such was his transformation. To this day, he is still a vital contributor at his organization, one of the top three payment services firms in the world.

The Turnaround

Another scenario I recall was being interviewed for a role within an industry I had only been on the periphery of previously. The executive vice president (EVP) interviewing me began by explaining their business. My inexperience in the industry troubled me and I raised my hand to point out that while I totally understood the environment and solutions being discussed, I did not have direct experience of the space. The immediate response was "It does not matter."

I knew straightaway that something else was at stake here. As the EVP continued, I thought to myself "why am I sitting here?" and I concluded that it must be my experiences of building sales teams and cultures married to my enterprise and start-up experiences. This indeed turned out to be true. As I continued my interview process, meeting other senior leaders on the interview panel, I began to flesh out a picture of a business unit that had lost its way.

Leadership had recently changed; the direction was not aligned to the goals of the overall business and worse still, the team was isolated, dysfunctional, and not performing to its true potential. I was also told by another senior colleague on the interview panel that I would need to address some unspecified "people problems" as a priority.

Now, you may or may not discover or be told these things throughout an interview process for a turnaround situation. Perhaps, the management will tell you vague things like "the team is not performing" or "sales are not where we hope them to be." What to expect and what to consider in this scenario?

First, as pointed out earlier, do not prejudge or jump to conclusions; there could be salvageable situations and talents and it is only after you have met with the team and seen the dynamics up front that you can draw effective conclusions. It is so important in this scenario not to go in with preconceived ideas, as there are two sides to every story.

On this occasion, I asked to go in to meet the team a couple of weeks before officially joining, essentially to listen, to be on receive, and to draw my own initial conclusions on the scale of the challenge ahead. It was also to take some of the possible tension out of my first official day in the business. I also wanted to get a sense of who might be with me and if anyone would be oppositely inclined.

I sat with each team member for an hour. My goal was to get a sense of each person, to ask them about themselves, their lives, motivations, and concerns. The business had clearly gone through some things and I also wanted to get a sense of how the team perceived the status and viability of the mission. Their reflections I hoped would give me food for thought in the remaining period before I officially joined.

I also wanted to start to know my people holistically, not just in the work context but to sense their values and what they might or might not be looking for. I was also keen to share a sense of myself, my journey in work, my values, and my personal life. In any situation like this, you must be conscious that you yourself are of course also being evaluated and that people are equally trying to gain clues as to the future direction.

As predicted, these meetings gave me much to reflect on as I served the remainder of my notice period before joining. I could sense nervousness and it was instructional to note the degree of openness or lack thereof. There had even been some open hostility from one team member, which had shocked me.

Encountering outright hostility is always a shock, especially on a first meeting, as we all want to treat people as we would like to be treated ourselves, but knowing this was also in the environment was illuminating and now, I had some time to reflect before my start date on why this might be the case.

If you are entering a turnaround situation, you must prepare and expect to be dropped into a potentially hostile environment. Confrontation and difficult conversations can be an uncomfortable place for many of us, especially if someone has taken against you and you are not sure why. Conflict can be shocking and is not something we all like to meet head on. In the scenario I have outlined, you have to prepare yourself for some measure of conflict or, at the very least, awkwardness or tough conversations.

Try always to depersonalize anything involving heightened emotions. Whoever is treating you aggressively is not being personal; how could they be, especially if you have only just met them. There is clearly something else going on which they cannot fully communicate to you. What is more likely to be the case is that they are projecting onto you a fear or anger or even a deep-seated grievance. It is your job to figure out what this might be and whether the situation can be amicably resolved for the good of the business.

Remember, you are a totally unknown quantity to your team at this point. Reflect on the fact that for you to be there, the team have themselves experienced uncertainty and likely could be in mourning, due to lost aligned loyalty to the leadership which has now left. Trust will be low where you are concerned and you have to focus on building that. Resentment could also be stemming from feelings of having been passed over for promotion, or an attitude that you as the new entrant cannot possibly know as much as them, which honestly may well be true, especially about the specifics of a product or service. Be conscious of this: it is never about what you do not know, it's always about why you were hired to do the job in the first place.

"Weaponized" information in this context is when an individual starts knowingly or unknowingly to act as a bottleneck. If this is done on purpose, it is because they have equated knowledge to equal power. This will be manifested by the effort to create a fiefdom and possibly to show up those around them. This can largely be a defensive mechanism born of a feeling that either people or even the organization is against them. When this is at play, the dominate person is unlikely to see that they are having an adverse effect on the wider team. They may indeed feel entirely righteous. They are likely to feel as if their expertise automatically garners respect onto them. What they are doing in reality is effectively preventing anyone else from leveling up. They are also probably intimidating the team around them, who may or may not be able to speak up about the situation. Be conscious of cultural dynamics at play here too.

All this happened to me for real and led to a scary but ultimately entirely fulfilling time as I had eventually to help this individual to be happy somewhere else. In so doing, I lost the most experienced and knowledgeable person in the team at that time and I knew we would all have to build again from scratch. This I resolved to do with my remaining team, to rebuild the entire group from the ground up, with support from international colleagues. I made a real effort to show the contrasts in how I wanted to see relationships and the business conducted. I focused hard on demonstrating my values in action. We also spent a lot of time in forging our internal team dynamics.

Looking back, all this made our team stronger. The experience forged us and we developed our expertise and remodeled approaches to serve the customers. Critically, we did this while totally resetting our approaches and collective culture. This was ultimately a business we doubled in under two years. Adversity can help to build the most cohesive units, instilling belief that if the worst can be overcome, anything is ultimately achievable.

The lesson here is that as hard as it is to acknowledge, you should always prepare yourself for people who may not be on the journey with you and to accept that this is also ok. We are inherently social beings who like to be liked; we can also be the heroes of our own narrative and find it hard to accept when others take against us. That often the most disruptive can also be currently the highest level performers in the team is unfortunate. This can on the face of it pose a real challenge and a danger of tribalism, with power structure silos emerging, undermining forces or worse. Try to identify these people early. Work to try and onboard them to your mission, values, and behaviors, but do not hesitate to help them to be happy somewhere else, if their actions are detrimental to the wider group.

As we have discussed elsewhere, single contributors can, quite literally, be exactly that: pure born hunters, focused only on bringing home the prey to the business to be rewarded and heralded as the great provider. Sometimes, these performers, while being totally effective, can also be incapable of sharing knowledge or being able to interact across the team.

I like to think of the sales team through the analogy of a car engine, where all components small or large are designed to hurtle you down the road toward your goal and your destination. When all are working in harmony, well oiled, by true alignment and fueled by accomplishment and success, the journey is smooth, fun, stress free, and exhilarating. The moment one of those engine components starts changing the rules or preventing the success of others, then the engine can quickly fall apart and a toxic culture can cause a total breakdown. You may break down or you may still make it to your destination, but the journey will not be pleasant either way.

It can be so challenging to consider helping the best performer or the most experienced and knowledgeable person move on. Try always to again share and attempt to bind these folks into your mission. This is why stating expected behaviors and values is as important as setting the financial and other sales metrics, because the how is as important as the result, if you are building something sustainable that will grow exponentially over the long term.

If you are letting someone go, always make it a point to celebrate their contributions collectively. I would always make a special effort to honor those leaving with the whole team. Make a point to genuinely express the sadness of not being able to learn from them and their experience. The team is important. In showing that it is uppermost in your mind, you will again be sending strong messages to the group, particularly to those remaining.

The key is that every time I have witnessed this, the remaining team has never looked back. Once culture is formulating or set, you must jealously look after it, as it is a fragile thing. It is better to think that the work of culture building is never really complete. If you do, you will have a chance to build something self-sustaining that helps to attract the types of talent that you want to maintain your growth. It is really true that a rising tide lifts all boats.

The New Start

When one is hiring and building a team from scratch, you have a completely blank canvas, which should allow for the screening of candidates based not only on their experience but also on their understanding of the environment they will join, as well as their soft skills.

It should also be easier to define and set the ball rolling on the culture. Keeping an eye on how this develops as you build your team does remain critical. Be conscious of the maturity of the organization as you develop. At the beginning, you are probably seeking go-getters who can thrive in nebulous environments; this is key when sales and revenue trumps all else. Later down the track, you will need to supplement these folks with experience and enhanced processes, as you mature out approaches to market. This is the point where you may need to be conscious of needing to evolve the culture to fit the new requirements.

Sources of Conflict

Disagreements and debates at work are healthy and indicative of a passionate and diverse culture. When passionate and talented people come together, you can expect spirited debate and points of view to be exchanged. Authentic leaders will encourage this. The key is to wed these dynamics to universally accepted values of respect and specifically to the building bridges to win behavior. It is crucial that people recognize that this is an integral aspect of your business approach and that they adhere to these principles collectively. Ensure that all interaction of this type is centered around clear objectives and aligned goals in the market. If you have not centered in these ways, you are likely to only foster chaos and competing tracts of activity, likely with very limited focus.

Disagreements can, sometimes, escalate into conflict. Unresolved conflict can easily spread from the individuals to inflect the wider team and ultimately your culture. We have all witnessed or heard of toxic cultures and siloed fiefdoms of power in the workplace. In my opinion, this is often based on a lack of clear and aligned mission across the group. It is also likely that the values and expected behaviors of the organization or group have not been fully articulated or set.

It can also be about a loss of direction. Disagreements or lengthy debate without a sense of shared accessible plans to capture, prioritize, and solve the issue, whether it be through approaches to market, product development, or something else, can lead to disillusionment for the entire company project. In my experience, this is usually indicative of an environment where there are challenges with the proposition in the market. Entire meetings can disassemble into some lengthy micro discussions on some small facet of the solution. Descent into unstructured debate never helps to identify clear priorities of where to play and how to win.

As a commercial leader, be careful to recognize this phenomenon should it occur. Make sure to clearly capture the issues and what the cost or impacts might be in terms of not addressing the observable opportunities. Make sure these are well presented and aligned with colleagues in other functions and that there is some accountability to formulate solutions. If allowed to persist, not only can such endless debates be thoroughly demotivating and lead to talent flight risks, but the core issues for failing in the market might also not be fully understood by company leadership.

The longer this is allowed to continue, the more demotivating collective meetings can become and this lack of morale can quickly seep into the culture. Leadership must be able to spot the tipping point of healthy debate and sharing of ideas before it becomes something potentially harmful. Here, you, as the commercial leader, must step in to bring the voice of the market to the needs of the solution. Make sure to confer this responsibility clearly to your team so that good data and market-based stories can be captured and presented clearly.

To be clear, not every proposition in the market will be fully evolved to solve for potential customer needs. Enhancements and development are necessary and are a result of activity in the market, whether in response to a competitor feature or because of a customer request. There will always be differentials across competing propositions in market. The key is that your team has faith that they know what to sell, how to sell, and how to position the value proposition to win more times than they lose. Aligned to that they need faith that their feedback is heard and that there is a plan to enhance or solve for any challenges being thrown up. Decluttering the go-to market is a key aspect in all of this.

Ensure that all commercial functions map out and know what the value propositions and use cases are. In addition, if the sales team is not capturing vital market information in a structured way to be shared and discussed with product and other functions, then that itself is a problem that needs to be fixed asap. Setting in place cross-functional processes, highlighting the intent or plan, is something to execute on as soon as your culture is risked by less-open and fractious team dynamics.

I really do see this as the responsibility of the commercial sales leader to ensure a clear go-to market strategy is developed and aligned across all functions. Getting closer to defining winning use cases matched to market potential is vital to be able to help support all parts of the company pulling together in the same direction. The entire commercial team should be coached to represent the market opportunity in total, not simply what is pipeline-ready today. Research, or T-shirt-sizing the overall market, should meet on the ground definition of observable opportunity, which should be clearly housed in the customer relationship management (CRM) system. Remember that these inputs will also form part of your future rocket fuel predictions on where your business could be, in the coming years.

Conflict in a sales environment can be a product of a few common factors. Be on the lookout for these:

- Lack of clarity of role or function—that is, confusion about how to be successful/make money.
- Lack of clarity around pay and commission.
- The formation of cliques or subcultures—at worse leading to weaponized information.
- Unhealthy competition or the perception of favoritism— the elevation of single contributors.
- A confused product alignment to market.
- A confused, ill-defined go-to market approach.
- A lack of communicating customer and/or market needs in the organization.

Be conscious that sources of conflict may not only reside in your team and could equally come from the following;

Other Functions

If there is conflict with other functions, then it likely again stems from a lack of alignment between you and the other department's counterpart. This is why sharing and aligning your plans with other functions is vital to ensure that you are on the same path and direction. Therefore, as part of developing your strategy and go-to market plans, I would encourage that these are shared with other relevant functional leaders at an early stage to gain this alignment, as well as any feedback you can gather and incorporate.

The clear principle is that, first, all elements of the leadership team should be aligned, and should be actively collaborating to win for the business and, second, all customer-owning functions should share their customer obsession and collaborate well together as a team, to improve service and develop opportunity in the market. The cornerstone one-page plan, which we will explore later, is the tool that you can use to do this in a clear, structured fashion.

Other Leaders

Senior leaders may also be single contributors in function and not directly manage teams or territories. As such, they may not see people dynamics in the same way you do.

Again, open collaboration and alignment is critical. Spend time to understand their motivations and what they are driving in their functions. Sharing your plans will enable you to identify where you have initiatives in common, allowing you to work together in greater harmony.

Hiring Plans

Ensuring that your hiring plan supports and enhances your organizational culture is critical for building a cohesive and aligned team.

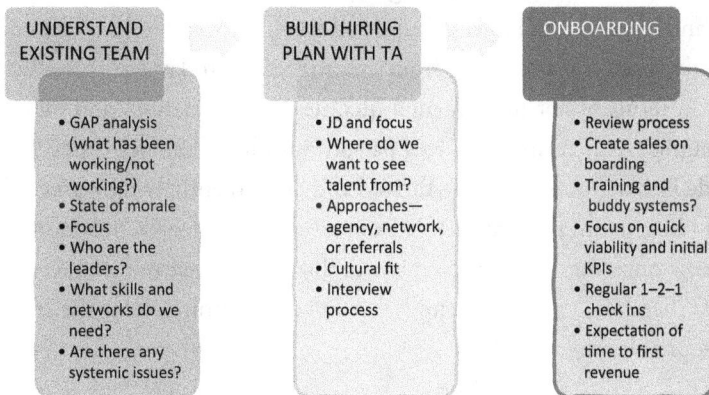

UNDERSTAND EXISTING TEAM	BUILD HIRING PLAN WITH TA	ONBOARDING
• GAP analysis (what has been working/not working?) • State of morale • Focus • Who are the leaders? • What skills and networks do we need? • Are there any systemic issues?	• JD and focus • Where do we want to see talent from? • Approaches—agency, network, or referrals • Cultural fit • Interview process	• Review process • Create sales on boarding • Training and buddy systems? • Focus on quick viability and initial KPIs • Regular 1–2–1 check ins • Expectation of time to first revenue

Figure 6.1 Hiring plan template

Strategically integrate your organizational culture into the hiring process. Not only do you want to attract individuals who align with your values, but also you want to be fostering an environment where the employees thrive and contribute positively to the overall culture you are building.

Figure 6.1 represents the steps you may want to consider when discussing and creating a hiring plan for your team. Be sure to discuss, align, and agree with your HR and/or Talent Acquisition partner.

I would strongly advise, when building a team culture, to directly involve your team in the hiring process to check cultural fit. As an example, when in a commercial leadership role in Singapore, I had to hire for a technical engineer, someone whose focus was also customer facing, though concentrating on the demonstration and implementation of our software solutions at the time. The person I shortlisted came highly recommended. I could tell she had the attributes that would allow her to thrive in our "start-up" environment, where ambiguity was high; support, including training, for her role was low; and where a self-starting, solutioning mindset plus customer and team obsession were key. The challenge was I could not clearly understand her. This meant that I was conflicted, yet my gut was telling me that this was the right person. The team liked her too, as I had asked them to screen her in their own one-to-one interviews as well. I trusted my team, but had to overcome my own barriers to the selection.

I resolved to call on one of her ex-managers. I told him that I was concerned that I might be leaning toward a decision that was more about me and less about the role, culture, and team. He told me he understood exactly where I was coming from and proceeded to lay my concerns to rest in terms of her fundamental qualities, determination, and cultural strengths. As it turned out, this person was one of the best hires I ever made into a group, ever. She thrived and created entirely new processes, including pathways that enabled our overall customer acquisition and success once they were implemented. Taking yourself out of the equation, therefore, can sometimes be an important principle in the service of your culture.

So, consider that hiring a new person to fit seamlessly into the cultural jigsaw puzzle involves a thoughtful and strategic approach. Here's how you can serve your culture and achieve impactful, successful hiring:

1. *Define cultural components*:
   - Clearly identify the key components of your organizational culture. This may include values, communication styles, collaboration preferences, and other aspects that contribute to the overall workplace atmosphere.
2. *Integrate cultural fit into job descriptions*:
   - Explicitly mention your company's culture in job descriptions. Clearly communicate the values and attributes that you're looking for in a candidate to attract individuals who resonate with your organizational ethos.
3. *Incorporate culture into your interviews*:
   - Develop interview questions that assess a candidate's alignment with your cultural values. Behavioral interview techniques can be particularly effective in gauging how candidates have demonstrated cultural compatibility in their previous roles.
4. *Involve multiple stakeholders*:
   - Include various team members, especially those who embody your culture, in the interview process. Their perspectives can provide valuable insights into how well a candidate is likely to integrate into the existing cultural dynamics.
5. *Transparently share your culture*:
   - Personally, I will only do this when or if a candidate asks. If asked during interviews and the hiring process, I would always be transparent about my company culture. Clearly articulate what it's like to work in your organization and the behavioral expectations that contribute to a positive cultural fit.
6. *Assess adaptability*:
   - While cultural fit is crucial, also assess a candidate's adaptability. They should be able to integrate into your culture while bringing a fresh perspective and contributing positively to the team dynamics.

7. *Reference checks with culture in mind*:
 • When conducting reference checks, inquire about how
   candidates have thrived in or contributed to the cultures of
   their previous workplaces. This can provide additional insights
   into their cultural compatibility.

By intentionally incorporating cultural concerns throughout the
hiring process, you increase the likelihood of finding individuals, who
not only meet your desired skill sets, but also seamlessly integrate into and
enhance your organizational culture.

> *Authentic leadership is about being available, present, and interested in
> your people beyond the mission.*

Takeaways

 • *Find out "who's who in the zoo."*
 • *Be aware of previous dynamics and loyalties and observe how
   people are showing up and interacting.*
 • *Observe what current dynamics are at odds with the values
   and culture you want to build.*
 • *Tie everything back to winning in the market, to your
   mission, and to your customers—build customer obsession.*
 • *Do not take challenging moments or emotions personally.*
 • *Always prepare well and ask for permission to have a tough
   conversation when needed.*
 • *Always remember that not everyone will be with you on the
   journey and that this is ok.*
 • *Hire with a cultural emphasis.*

CHAPTER 7

The Sales Team

Chapter Summary

- Sales teams have particular dynamics; be conscious of these and of what is driving success and what potentially is holding you back.
- Culture needs emphasis and focus; this chapter underscores the pivotal role of behaviors and values in cultivating a high-performance sales culture, driven by excellence and achievement.

I used to think the very term "sales team" was something of a misnomer, perhaps because I began my career in a very specific and aggressive commission-only sales environment, where I witnessed my "boiler room" moments, and my first sales teams always seemed to be filled with the most outlandish and incredibly strong, individualistic characters.

Later in my career, as I sought to improve on my sales skills, I would always seek out the best-performing individuals across the organization to try and learn from their approaches, so as to adapt good learnings into mine. I was always interested in the storytellers—those who really listened to and intelligently questioned their prospects or customers and who would then weave a narrative in the customer's language, using the names of their team players in relation to the product or service being sold. Within this research and learning, I would always find it instructive as well when I came across those who were closed to sharing the secrets to their success.

Storytelling, in the context of sales, for me, is the ability to verbally embed the product or solution being sold into the client's universe, by connecting their language to the features, benefits and value, being presented. In essence, storytelling in sales is about creating a narrative that engages, informs, and persuades. It is a powerful tool for turning supply into partnership, as strong relationships can be built on the sense that this provider truly understands the issue being solved for. I made sure I cast my net wide to glean insights from experts in various functions in the business, facilitating a deeper understanding of the most effective contributors for specific deals. Recognizing that success in sales is a collective effort, I believe in the idea that when sales wins, everybody wins. Hence, collaboration becomes a key strategy for collective victories.

I believe there was a time when managements would actively seek and coach singular hunter behaviors in their teams. This was reflected in the sales training of the day: objection handling and close loop techniques. One of the most famous courses of the time was IBM sales training. This was before the days of consultative selling, later challenger or value-selling schools of thought, and literally reflected the process to sell a piece of hardware, which was their heritage and focus at the time, now long since reinvented. Find the objection, isolate it, put it down, move to close. Repeat. Keep on as long as it would take to gain commitment and a deal. This was about features and benefits within a singular sales approach.

You might say the same of cold calling within the context of certain financial or insurance services, which is the industry in which I cut my teeth. Within these environments, sales is about numbers and funnel metrics. So many calls result in so many meetings and so many sales. In that sense, the sales collective is managed in quite a singular fashion. You meet the KPIs, you do the numbers, and you win.

Today, the more applied skills of leading with value propositions, collaboration, integrated partnership, knowledge sharing, and team-first principles are rightly at the forefront and they match a more consultative and partnership approach to selling. This is also translated into the existing customer base where selling is about the sticky, value-added relationship. Focusing on the whys of a deal is a more rigorous and often total company approach to selling, but that has not signified the death of the single contributor—far from it.

Within any organization and across all functions, individuals who fiercely protect their intellectual property (IP), and business knowledge persist. This reality is alive and thriving. Additionally, the scarcity of investment in sales training by many companies, coupled with a dearth of knowledge sharing and collaboration within or between sales teams, creates an atmosphere where individuals must autonomously seek solutions to flourish. Transformation in such environments occurs only when a coaching mentality is instilled from leadership, accompanied by genuine prioritization and emphasis on this approach.

Now, for a health warning. I have been a sportsperson throughout my life and am an avid sports fan in my free time. I will use a couple of these experiences to illustrate points. Sports after all is a high-performance environment where teams and individuals rise and decline, where culture and incremental gains are vital, and where the most important talents are the individual components of the team. So, please see the message and do not be turned off by mention of cricket, football, or car engines as much as possible. I, for my part, will endeavor not to labor the points!

I used to play cricket at a decent standard, which is not going to be everyone's cup of tea I understand, but hang in there and bear with me. Cricket is often described as a team game, though I would often equate cricket and sales teams as quite similar animals. Cricket is actually quite individualist. The key duel boils down to a bowler and a batsman. The bowler is singularly in a one-to-one campaign against the batsman; each ball is a battle. Of course, there is a specialist team surrounding them, but this is where the core action is taking place. This is often the way in sales teams also; within the campaign of your sales year, each individual battle to win a deal is usually helmed by one salesperson; of course, again there is a surrounding team, but it is the focus of one individual to bring in the deal.

Ultimately, in cricket, a group of individual performers combine to win. Often walking out to bat or in the field, I would be struck at how much the "team" was bickering or seemingly at odds with one another. If their attentions were focused on you or toward an opposition batsman, then you would be entering a pretty hostile environment. Intra team bickering was not at all unusual, especially at club level, as again competitive spirits would be coming together and that is not always a smooth process. I would imagine the opposition would find this most disconcerting but then they were likely no different than us! My reflection of many sales teams I have been a part of is that this is really no different. Sales teams are also often made up of specialists in either market or product and if they are not harnessed well together, the individualistic qualities can outweigh the collective very easily. It should also be said that some leadership personalities and management cultures like to foster and even encourage such dynamics. Sometimes this is very conscious, sometimes it is unintentional, or a pure reflection of the dominant leader's personality.

Expectations, corporate cultures, and management have changed no doubt since the start of my career until now, but I can think of many so-called teams which were really no more than a group of high-performing individuals, jealously guarding and pursuing their own business, without any sense of a collective to be seen. This is almost always in environments where the full expectation of delivery is placed on the sales team and usually where there is no wider plan or strategy beyond this.

This can often lead to talented individuals being left isolated and under supported. It is also more often than not a major contributor to toxic work environments. In fact, leadership can often work to intensify competition across the group, which is unlikely to produce sustaining, growing teams, as turnover and focus on the number are the more likely imperatives.

Be conscious of your product and the metrics that drive success. In some environments, key performance indicator (KPI)-driven approaches can of course make sense, especially if combined with a coaching method. Recruitment is an industry where this approach thrives and where turnover of placements is critical; therefore focused activity is a key driver to success. If you work in environments with longer deal cycles and complex offerings that drive value at a client, then fostering a team dynamic and culture will always win out long term over a pure volume, funnel, pipeline-driven approach to management. As a new sales manager, however, it can seem daunting to put the needs of the collective above the P&L contribution of a single individual.

As a first time sales leader, I was thrust into just such a collective of strong, in the main successful, single contributors. The jealous holding onto their business IP behavior was now extended to me, the perceived ex team member, as I was now viewed as management. How is one to build or improve anything if the pursuit is so individualistic? Thus began my journey into considering how to bring together such groups toward a goal greater than themselves and how to foster deeper collaboration on the path to greater achievements. Perhaps, I was into my third or fourth sales leadership position before I began to think of the sales team as you would of a high-performance sports engine—you can insert here whichever brand you would like.

The Sales Team as High-Performance Engine

An engine is filled with small and larger components; there is no wastage and nothing is idle. Each component is expert in its function and together, when operating optimally, they combine to hurtle you toward your destination. Slow and steady or with exhilarating speed, the team works together to achieve the outcome. I have also heard revenue termed as the "exhaust of sales," but let's not stretch the analogy too far!

What happens if you remove a component? I'm certainly no engineer but even the smallest component can break your vehicle if it malfunctions. I once had a car where an incident with the water pump or filter (I told you I was nontechnical) exploded and took out the cam belt (a pretty necessary item to drive an engine), which led to an immediate, terminal electrical and engine cut-out. Utterly catastrophic. I was coasting on my 80-mph momentum only, with no way to show hazards, indicate or moderate my speed other than to break. Seeing as I was in the fast lane on a motorway and fast approaching a traffic jam, this was less than ideal.

The smallest component had destroyed the whole and I was now fire-fighting, seeking a safe way off the busy lanes of traffic, eventually making my way to the hard shoulder. It is the same for your sales culture. I think all of us in sales have also been in situations where there has been a sensation of complete loss of control and the longer you are in sales, the more likely for you to encounter this scenario at some time or another.

The Fragility of Culture

Cultures and smooth-running teams are very fragile things. We only have to look to our favorite sports teams to see a litany of rising and falling fortunes, in spite of and sometimes because of the talented individuals collected together. How many times in football (soccer, the real football), for example, have we seen the scenario of a manager clashing with a star player, a talent deemed too good to drop. The stakes are exponentially higher for the manager because if he exerts discipline and drops this superstar, the knives will be out if things go badly. It is educational though, how many times letting the star go, ends up with the entire team leveling up in the end—even a superstar whose cultural impact is only positive. Again, if handled well, the collective can raise their standards and outputs based on a shared responsibility and pride in performance.

Sometimes, an outstanding performer can also be holding the entire team back through selfish actions and the atmosphere they create as dominate personalities. While it is usually not easy to consider helping a star performer be happier somewhere else, such individualism can be truly damaging to the group. As we have discussed, I have witnessed on many occasions that once the individual has either chosen to leave of their own accord, or been encouraged to, the watermark of the entire team has lifted. No one individual is ever larger than the collective. The key is collective responsibility. A level-playing field and a happier, more constructive culture, can make dramatic impacts on a team not performing to its true potential.

This is why acquisitions can be so tricky for both the acquiree and the acquirer. It is inevitable that at some point in your career you will experience this from one perspective or the other. The culture of the two groups and how the leaderships turn up can have either a freeing or very damaging impact on the collective. Moments like these need careful monitoring of the people situation, as the talent may vote with their feet and you could find yourself losing great people in the process, not to mention the shockwaves that may enter the market.

I have had too many experiences to recount here about this process and misaligned cultures, perhaps even enough for another book! The needs of the business and the needs of the collective culture need careful consideration when bringing these groups together. Be sure to plan accordingly and to be aligned to HR and your management.

Once developed, a team or culture and the sets of behaviors that make them are to be guarded and never taken for granted. It always starts with the people. It takes hard work and dedication to assemble and keep a team. Never take it for granted. History abounds with the rise and fall of great teams, but if you guard and police what is important, you can maintain and thrive in your culture throughout any circumstances. Ultimately, by identifying the leaders in your group and working closely with them, you can get to a self-policing environment. That said, you must keep it fresh and ensure that you are always working to bind the group to the goals you are setting. This is why it is vital to identify and map your talent and potential leaders in the group early. Arsène Wenger was the longest serving manager of the Arsenal football club from 1996 to 2018 and became the most successful in the club's history. His take on team spirit and culture is illustrative of the point:

> *Therefore, I believe it's a little bit like a flower. You have to take care of it and look after it every day, or else it will slowly die. But as well, you can make the flower bigger, better and prettier if you care for it.*
> —Arsène Wenger, Copyright © 2024 The Arsenal Football Club Limited. www.arsenal.com.

So, go back to the reference of your high-performing sales team as a car engine. You have to know each component intimately, what motivates them, what makes them tick, and what gets them up and to work every day. It is only through knowing the individuals that you can understand how they work and how to best help them to deliver explosive growth.

Just like an engine you will inherit key team members. You have to consider how they interact with the other components. Is there sharing and collaboration? Do all celebrate together? Discover who is aligned to whom and how do they present to other customer-facing parts of the organization. Do all learn together, whether from defeat or victory? Or do the gears grind with friction? Be conscious of friction. Ongoing tension and silos wear people out and ultimately lead to breakdown.

A good engine also needs fuel and it needs oil to grease the motions and provide efficiency. The fuel in this instance can be the collective alignment to *one* goal and the desire to win and celebrate together. This should also include those on the technical, delivery and support side.

The sense of a shared mission and purpose aligned to personal goals can then become a companywide experience. Individual goals are made more powerful if they are also personal in nature or carry an element bound to the individual's learning and growth. If managed simply by metrics or too delivery focused, then they can ultimately be less sticky. The oil in this analogy might stand for shared knowledge: efficiency brought through a growth mindset facilitated by coaching and mentorship, to take market expertise and approaches to the next level across the group.

> *When curiosity toward people meets a common aligned plan within a safe psychological environment, you begin to have the components that make behavior-driven culture.*

So many leaders focus only on the P&L or have an inauthentic approach to the people sides of their business. Such environments can see great swings in performance, burn out, and team turnover. People want to be able to see their contributions and how they impact the business. They also want to feel valued. Leadership that does not engage and that is not visible, will have an impact on culture over time. Executives who lock themselves away in their offices and seem only to engage with their executive group are classic examples of this.

You cannot delegate culture build; everyone needs to live and breathe the common purpose, otherwise you risk the sense of being an inauthentically directed company, as opposed to a collectively managed one. Behaviors like this can really serve to undermine a culture. Great places to work are built through engagement at all levels, to the mission, and to the values recognized and celebrated.

Ensure that common "soft" KPIs are built in at all layers of the company, which focus on cultural behaviors and values. These could be delivered as part of the annual review process, whereby an element of performance is geared toward values such as "winning it together." Also ensure that 360 degree and step feedback processes are in place, as part of six-monthly formal reviews, as this again shows that the company is backing itself to live and breathe its published principles at all levels.

Finally, reflect on the statement "behaviors form culture leading to results," as a belief statement to help you crystalize the philosophy of the change and focus you will bring as a leader. Think about what that means to you and how that might be brought to life by you in your organization and with what results.

Takeaways

- *The engine needs to run smoothly and needs maintenance.*
- *Establish what your values and key approaches are—set these down.*
- *Find your leaders—today's and tomorrow's.*
- *Communicate goals and priorities aligned to behaviors.*
- *Live and breathe your culture.*
- *Pay continued attention to developing your culture at all times.*
- *Keep it fresh and ensure the strategy, direction, and focuses are clearly known and referred to at all times.*

CHAPTER 8

Managing Difficult Personalities

Chapter Summary

- *In various scenarios such as the promotion and the turnaround, you are likely to have to manage your relationship with more challenging personalities or behaviors.*
- *As you bed down your culture, keeping diverse, talented, and ambitious people together and aligned to the values, behaviors, and set outcomes of your mission can at times be challenging.*
- *In this chapter, we focus on handling difficult conversations in the best way to allow the team and at times yourself to get back on track.*

Throughout the course of any career, you can guarantee that you will come across and will often have to lead or manage some people who are more difficult than others.

If you have spent some critical time in defining the way you intend to go about your business as a group, you will also go a long way to understanding who is truly with you on the journey as well as creating frameworks to help you manage those who might, for whatever reason, be misaligned to this particular goal. Diversity of thought—a safe environment for anyone to speak up in—is what you should strive for, but if this becomes divisive, distracting, damaging, and/or toxic, then you must work to resolve the situation fast. Competitive and strong-minded people pulling together in one direction is ultimately the winning dynamic to achieve. Connecting your people to the mission is the rocket fuel of your group dynamic.

Culture and belief in the mission is the glue. The culture and values of an organization have to be lived, breathed, and upheld by all. When setting cultural goals, be careful that you are not merely paying lip service to the exercise. It is no good for a leadership group to announce a set of values without them being articulated and breathed through the management layers and onward through the organization. Stated but unlived behaviors and values at best come off as insincere; at worst, they can undermine belief in your organization. This is especially so if added to an aloof leadership and bad news or results. This is why behaviors and values will form a key part of your cornerstone plan and should be articulated and celebrated alongside the targets and focuses for your group.

If you do not have set values and behaviors within your organization, you will find that a department or sales organization will fall whim to the power of the leader's personality and style. Inauthentic business styles of leadership will often lead to an unengaged team, and retention could be a real issue. In this type of environment, newly promoted sales leaders can often find themselves in a sink or swim environment, especially if they have leaders above them who cannot help themselves in getting constantly involved. Not being left alone and supported in doing their jobs can effectively undermine the commercial leader's position. This is why many newly promoted sales managers may find themselves moving on within a year.

The Stress of Confrontation

We all react to people in different ways. Challenging people can be both positive and negative. As a sales leader, you have to give of yourself equally and find ways to be a better communicator across the board. You will not always be able to bring everyone on the journey with you; that is a fact. Sometimes, especially in turnaround situations, you will also find yourself perhaps in toxic environments.

Confrontation is not a bad thing. Difficult and frank discussions are a necessary part of business. However, it is when these dialogues spill over into hostility or when communications completely break down that the problems can start. It's all about a loss of control: that feeling that you are not being or acting like yourself, because you feel that you cannot adequately communicate with an individual or that they are steamrolling you, or that they are simply not even open to your point of view.

How we deal with confrontation is a deeply personal matter and it is good to build some self-awareness around this topic. It is also good to get a read on how certain team members make you feel in the moment, so that you can prepare yourself to be the best you can be in any contentious day-to-day dealings you may encounter.

I once had a colleague who would obliterate with feedback, an incessant talker. At that moment, I would realize that I was not my usual articulate self and unable to find a common ground or solution. I would find his arguments unimpeachable at that moment, even though I felt that my point of view or vision was not being seen or heard. I would often find myself shut down, incapable of accessing the facts and counterpoints that would allow me to have a full two-way dialogue. I would often have to frequently and forcibly interject to interrupt his flow. My mind and my language would be blank. What I did not realize at the time was that I was panicking.

If this happens to you, it is essentially your fight or flight in full effect. The moment is intensified and you may notice heightened heartbeat and sweaty palms, likely an adrenaline spike. You are being confronted. Of course, not all confrontation is bad, some are inspiring and spur you onto greater focus or effort. This is largely when you are in a relationship you trust, because you know you can have a free-flowing, open, two-sided dialogue and you know you are heard and respected. However, when it is with someone you have difficulties with, it can get in the way of you communicating at your best.

If this is something that you observe, it is important to know what is going on physically and mentally at that moment. If you do not actively work on this, you will likely allow it to perpetuate and this particular relationship is likely to become toxic at some point. The worst you can do is to avoid that individual or to not isolate and acknowledge what you are feeling.

Just as you did when taking on your role, find some time and ask yourself open questions about what you are feeling without trying to solve for the situation at this point. Learn to be kind to yourself by first recognizing and then acknowledging that the fight or flight response is being triggered. You are likely panicked by being entirely conscious that you are not performing as you would optimally like to, that the situation is getting beyond you, and that you are being railroaded. You'll have the alert setting of your mind flashing peak emergency red; you have lost your words and therefore control of the situation.

Knowing something of your brain science here can help. In shutting down your anxiety responses, you have to be aware of being triggered into the fight, flight, or hide modality. Say to yourself "I am safe, I am calm, this is my body preparing for fight or flight." Just taking that moment can take the sting out of a situation, allowing you to collect yourself to identify and focus on a way to resolve the differences or specific challenges you are facing.

You should also observe and learn the responses you are feeling so you can divert your natural impulses and make a more constructive space for you to manage the situation. You can literally trick yourself by stepping into an alternative truth. For example, I actually always liked the person I am describing and who gave me so much difficulty. We had much in common and enjoyed many convivial moments, which is why the whole thing was entirely infuriating. Use such positive aspects to remember the person as opposed to the scenario in front of you and to try to bring matters back to basics. By doing so, you will begin to rewire the neutral pathways, so you are not so distracted in the moment. It is all about finding a counterpoint to the dynamics you feel with the individual right now, so that you might better manage matters.

At the same company, I had an executive who was playing three-dimensional chess when I was usually playing checkers. This individual was one of the most inspiring leaders I have come across and intellectually was always three to four steps or PowerPoint slides ahead of me at any given time. But I *loved* that. It made me raise my game every time. I was always better prepared and superengaged in those meetings. So, it often confused me why I could not engage the positive aspects of stress and performance when confronted by other challenging colleagues. Again, try to transpose the element that engages your competitive spirit to help in positively solving for those more difficult encounters you may have.

Tabling a Difficult Conversation

Sometimes it is necessary to table a frank and difficult conversation. As a leader, this initiative starts with you, either to begin a dialogue, "why is this not working in your opinion?" or to table a more formal conversation, whereby it is better to prompt that you need to have a frank dialogue and to ask whether this is a good time to do that.

Once you have reached a point where a more thorough examination of the matter, requiring collaborative effort, is necessary, it is advisable to express this need explicitly. By doing so, you are pre-emptively informing the other party of the nature of the upcoming conversation. This approach can minimize surprise, fostering a more open and less defensive atmosphere. The goal is to set a conducive tone and environment for initiating the dialogue.

Be well prepared and find a moment when both can be at their best for a focused conversation. In these moments, it is important to let the other person feel heard, listened to, and to allow them to air their side of the issue. When tackling a difficult conversation, one should strive to be clear, explain the situation as you see it, especially the impacts the behaviors are having on yourself or others around you. Sharing detail about the impact and feelings of the other's actions can show your interest and commitment to solving the issue. One should do this without emotion entering the conversation and the entire thing should be approached in an open and safe manner without accusation. Ask for their support to help resolve the issue and listen to their feedback; work to gain a consensus, if possible, on the path to communicating a clear resolution or a set of mutually accountable actions that can be agreed between the parties. These should be time bound and involve regular check-ins.

It is important to keep the conversation on track and focused toward the issue you are trying to raise and resolve. The final part of holding one another accountable to the actions and behaviors that you set for one another going forward is vitally important. If you cannot come to conclusions or solutions right away, table a follow-up that gives both parties time to consider and reflect. Again, focus this on the resolutions, as you do not want people to go away resentful and focused on injustice as they may see it.

Communicating Feelings

Communicating feelings can be especially hard, but one should be as clear as possible in terms of the impact of what was felt. This description should be layered for it to be fully understood and to land with the other person. Anything vague or woolly will not work. Impacts are important to convey as these are the reasons why the issue needs to be resolved in the first place.

One technique, when you have it, is to use the cornerstone plan. Call backs to the mission you have set, the values and behaviors you have agreed for the team, and your own values and belief systems can also set the tone for the discussion. Basing it on the cornerstone can also help to take emotion out of the conversation. Ask what support you can give to help and together agree on measurable, time-based actions you can both be accountable for. As leaders, we have to go first in creating and managing these moments in the context of building and maintaining the culture we are driving. Being a sales leader and building culture is so much about raising the potential and performances of those around you, including your own. You are enabling people to do the best that they can, day by day, with clear purpose toward your vision of the goals set by the business. Identifying challenges and issues and going first to resolve them are the essence of good leadership.

Ensuring that continuous feedback is a part of the culture is also important. Feedback is an essential part of growth and development. It is also something you should be open to and actively seeking in terms of your own performance. Not all of it will be positive on your journey and not everyone will be aligned with you or will agree with you. It is about bringing diverse individuals and ideas along with you in a consensus. Finding those points where you do agree is the best step to identifying whether you can find a way forward, based on some agreed principles and actions, or whether you have someone who unfortunately will not be on the extended journey with you.

If the matter is sufficiently contentious or if one has tried and failed to resolve the difference, then do not be afraid to call in a mediator, whether a senior leader or even HR. The approach outlined can of course only work if both sides are sufficiently committed to the company, the direction, and the set strategy, including the culture itself. If the person is not engaging or refuses to open up and continues their behaviors, then mediation is going to be necessary and helpful. If this is the scenario, then possibly there will be an exit for that individual.

Creating a Win–Win

Identifying and fostering win–win scenarios not only helps to strengthen team cohesion, but also cultivates the culture of mission-led collaboration, binding individuals together through shared success and a collective commitment to achieving set goals. This is what we are striving to do as salespeople when in front of our customers after all. So it is the same with our team and colleagues. As a sales person, you are trying to help your customer win. Identifying how is half the battle. Within a sale, you are looking to figure out where your value proposition is strongest. Is it a process efficiency, a cost saving, an enhancement, and will it match up to the buyer's internal goals and help them to advance? Whatever it is, you are seeking to align your language, company, product, service, culture, and goals to those of the customer. You must do the same with your colleagues. In sales leadership, you are seeking to bind your group together in the common understanding, belief, and ultimately celebrated achievement of your set and delivered goals.

Takeaways

- *Table that a difficult conversation is needed and remove the emotions.*
- *Explain, specifically, why the person's behaviors are affecting you, the team, or members in the team.*
- *Try to open up the other person's perspective.*
- *Gain a consensus that actions need to be taken through an open and safe dialogue.*

(Continued)

(Continued)

> - *Formulate a plan which marries to the values and behaviors you have set for the organization.*
> - *Hold one another accountable.*
> - *Place a timeline on action and review.*
> - *If there is still no outcome for the better, bring in a third party to help work out a plan.*
> - *Keep talking and seek to identify win–win scenarios to bind individuals to the mission.*

CHAPTER 9

Identifying Your Network

Chapter Summary

- As commercial leaders, we rarely allow ourselves time without distractions to analyze specific difficulties or challenges we may be facing.
- Consider leveraging your network in your leadership position to gain valuable insights, support, and collaborative opportunities that contribute to your overall effectiveness as well as your success.
- Consider the benefits of a formal executive coaching relationship in supporting your growth as a leader.
- Once familiar, seek out ways to incorporate coaching and mentorship approaches into your business as part of consolidating your culture and underpinning your commercial results.

An important priority in any organization is to identify those who can help you on your journey. This is about looking internally within your organization as well as externally, to find common cause, support, mentorship, or expertise.

Think of these connections as people you can learn from, who can advise or guide with an independent view, and who can support and/or provide aircover when needed. Having people you can bounce ideas off or check into for feedback on your journey is vital, and should be something you encourage your team to build as well. A connected, open and motivated team will stay together after all.

One of the greatest distractions for a commercial leader is constant escalation of day-to-day decisions. However, having a team which takes responsibility to solve for the challenges in front of you, before a final review or decision is made, allows the leader more time to think creatively about all aspects of the business. Looking around corners or future gazing is all the more harder if your view is constantly down in the trenches. Just as you should invest in building your organizational network, so should your team. Look at this aspect early on and see what you can do to help your colleagues find the connections and help they need in the wider business.

Your network should also be diverse and is something you should invest time in nurturing. Remember, though, a network is not something you should simply lean upon; it is something you must also serve. Being a good servant to your network will ensure that you in turn will receive support, as and when you need it.

Do not be afraid to ask for time with someone, no matter how senior, but do be clear on why you are asking and what you hope to gain from the meeting. When reaching out to somebody for the first time, be compelling in your outreach and state your goals clearly. If they are matched to those of the person you are approaching, then so much the better. Coffee, lunch, or cocktails are all learning environments where you can sit with someone and get their inputs or perspectives on an issue or challenge.

Curating a compelling outreach is all about research. Of course, we live in a time when doing some research on someone prior to approach is easily accomplished on the Internet, and can take you a long way toward helping you to pen a mutually compelling approach. Beyond the usual LinkedIn and social searches, think in terms of searching for any articles or posts that you can use to build the connection and mutual interest quickly.

Your network comprises of:

- Your reporting line and senior executive leaders.
- Executive supporters and sponsors—could be other board members or advisory partners.
- Fellow leaders of customer-facing functions.
- Friends in commerce and industry.
- Product, legal, and operations leaders.
- Experts in the organization.

- Professional external coaches and mentors.
- Your external network.
- The HR business partner.
- Marketing.
- Well-connected headhunters.

Think about your network in the following ways and connected to the value you can gain from them.

Your Reporting Line and Senior Executive Leaders

A sales leader should always be selling, both internally and externally. In that sense, I have always thought of the function as constantly advocating, and if you are not always pitching your business or your requirements to win, you are missing a vital element of your role. This means the need for constant communication and alignment. My advice to any sales leader would be to take any opportunity available to present your business to key stakeholders. However, do also be careful with your time management. It is very easy, especially if product is being formulated, to be sucked into numerous internal meetings that resolve little and focus nothing on the current sales effort, particularly the structuring of your go-to market engine.

Face-to-face communication is priceless. This is particularly vital if you are based or running a region remote from the HQ. Your first priority is to always align and gain buy-in from your immediate boss. The boss must be the first audience for your initial 90-day plan and your cornerstone plan, as and when you have developed these. Their buy-in and close support will be vital and you should ensure that you have carefully aligned your views and visions for and of the business with them. Having done this, seek to communicate these elements wider within your organization.

You should, for example, ensure that you have access to the next level of management or "step" leadership as it is sometimes referred to. Of course, your boss should be aware of and aligned to any meetings and discussions you may have in those forums. Ensure that you always feed back to them the high-level discussion points and any agreed outcomes when you do meet their boss or someone more senior. This is after all about polite sharing of data, perspectives, and outcomes across your cohort. None of this is about bypassing your direct-line manager. It is about furthering the goals of your business unit or function through visibility and aligned priorities. If you are working in a larger or multinational company, you may not often get this opportunity. When you or they are in town, make sure you formally book face-to-face time outside of the officially organized agenda. These moments are precious.

As you would with your immediate fellow functional leaders, when speaking to executive VP and above, ensure that you are using a tool, such as your cornerstone one-page plan, as the basis of the conversation. This provides you a summary structure and will support a jumping off point to discuss details or specifics regarding elements that you need support or investment in. Do not bring overly complex presentations or data for these types of meetings. Focus always on summary updates and those materials you need to be able to advance delivery or build the next revenue lines.

Executive Supporters and Sponsors

It is important to find senior leaders in the organization who are perhaps outside of your immediate reporting line that you can also use to bounce ideas off and garner support for the initiatives that you are keen to implement.

Just unpacking a challenge or an issue with someone interested, experienced, and not directly in your day-to-day reporting line, can be a helpful way of identifying and consolidating useful next steps and actions to help resolve or progress an issue. If aligned to your thinking, they can also help to progress your suggestions or agenda in decision-making forums that you are not directly a part of. In this interaction, asking more broad questions about the person's experience in handling a situation would be more advisable than going into heavy detail.

Fellow Leaders of Customer-Facing Functions

The leadership organization of every company is different, but it is not unusual for the leaders of every function to come together as part of an executive group to chart the path and progress of the organization toward its goals.

It is important to identify who within that group can support you in sales. This is most likely to be product, development, support, implementation, legal, marketing, and, of course, finance. In many stages of sales leadership, even the promotion scenario, but especially the turnaround or new start, it is not unusual for a sales leader to use these forums to educate others about the direction and focuses of the sales function. Do not assume this has been done clearly before. The cornerstone plan we are building toward is also the structured clear document you can use to deliver this agenda.

If, as leaders of your respective functions, you understand each other's focuses, goals, and challenges, then all are better equipped to come together in the service of the customer and the overall business outcomes you are aligned to deliver. Again, the cornerstone will provide you with a structured way to have this dialogue and to quickly surface areas to align on or develop further together.

Friends in Commerce and Industry

Ensure you are keeping across macro factors that might be affecting your business. Maintaining connections with friends in commerce and business is valuable for various reasons, including the potential for collaboration, knowledge exchange, business opportunities, and the cultivation of a supportive professional network that can contribute to mutual growth and success.

Product, Legal, and Operations Leaders

It is vital that you keep a strong relationship with these functions. Sales, product, and operations are all interconnected functions. Product and operations as functions are vital to the retention and expansion into customer opportunity. Operations is usually encompassing presales, implementation, and customer support. All three directly serve the client and should be close to the sales function. As part of a wider analysis into breaking new markets, you may well have discourse with your commercial legal function. As previously discussed, the first challenge is to ensure all are on the same page across these groups. Then, fact-based, data-driven dialogue can serve to move the needle in support of your strategy.

Sales leaders can provide insights from the field, such as customer feedback including market trends, which can all inform product improvements and adjustments, leading to aligned strategies to win in the market. Aligning with operations can help to make for more efficient customer onboarding and creates the potential to find additional revenue opportunity. The way to ensure you are gathering data is to ensure that you have thorough and structured win–loss analysis. Ensure not only that you build this into your CRM, but also that you are debriefing win–loss analysis well across your team. Create a centralized template to define the dollar opportunity when capturing anything missing in your product set. You may well have a sense of market size but adding the ground up view of the opportunity within your CRM by target customer, and if relevant, geography as well, allows you to cut and share this data internally in a structured way to support prioritization or allocation of resources to a development.

Work with these departments to ensure that there is a central single point of truth for gathering this data so that it does not get lost in a myriad of e-mails, chat, or text. There is nothing worse than trying to find reference to a deal and not recalling which channel the data is in. Ensuring that data is centralized will take discipline and time to make second nature, but this will ensure you save precious time when helping to prioritize the organization's efforts and investments on the next key elements of the roadmap.

The product roadmap should be frequently shared as well as tested against what each proposal is going to deliver in the market for sales. Therefore, ensure that you organize frequent opportunities for product to join your sales reviews and for the roadmap to be presented to the sales team within Q&A sessions.

Building relationships with leaders in other departments helps, therefore, to create a unified organizational vision. This alignment ensures that everyone is working toward common goals, fostering a sense of unity and shared purpose.

Experts in the Organization

People, passion, and products—the three ps that are the true assets of any organization in any field. Expertise and experience can be unlocked and you should find out who you can learn from, including who can assist you and your team in direct customer engagement.

This is all about having a learning mindset. Seeking out those who know the most about a market, product, or customer base, allowing us the opportunity to learn and improve about how we talk about our propositions, our products and our services.

This in turn allows you to have a coaching ear out for how your people communicate your offerings. Furthering your expertise enables you to be a more effective coach and mentor to those around you. With these insights, you will be better equipped to challenge or adapt the current focuses, or course correct approaches to customers in the market. Once you have identified your winning use cases to laser into, and your must-win or key customers, you can then play a more active role in supporting the efforts to win or expand in these accounts.

Identifying winning use cases and communicating these across your sales team is vital if you are in a phase where the product capabilities and the sales efforts are not aligned. This is where spending time with other experts in the business will help you to define exactly where to play and how to win. These use cases can be employed to focus activity, ensure quality pipeline build, and further translate customer wins into stories that enable the sales folks to take the language of a sector into the marketplace.

This is where your expertise must meet the rest of the company through updates and communication. Decluttering sales activity by applying focus into a number of defined winning use cases is definitely something that needs communicating beyond your team. Sharing with product to ensure their roadmap is helping you in the market and is aligned to the realities of the customer opportunity would be one priority. Sales can be a difficult place to be if management, product, and marketing are not aligned, and clearly bound to a north star of what the ambition is versus what the current market reality looks like. This interpretation and communication of the market has to be part of the sales leader's responsibility.

Professional External Coaches and Mentors

There is an important difference between an executive coach and a mentor. An executive coach will essentially avoid giving you suggested solutions. They will, however, guide you using models or tools to help you organize your thoughts, understand your emotions, and widen your perspectives on the route toward your finding the answers and solutions for yourself, which they will then hold you accountable to.

A mentor is more of an informal relationship, which you may develop either within or externally from your current organization. Mentors can offer a different type of guidance and support which is likely to be more solution based or directed toward direct career advice and career development discussions.

Within this section, I will focus more upon the executive coach relationship, which I would encourage any leader to investigate. Self-formulated solutions represent some of the most potent learning experiences available to us, and the confidence gained from successfully implementing an initiative you have devised is incredibly empowering.

Executive coaches are therefore, increasingly being seen as not only an investment in the development of leadership talent within companies, but also by extension an investment in a company's bottom-line. This is by no means a universal trend and does usually stem from a CEO or MD themselves having, and believing in the benefits of maintained executive coaching relationships. Having a growth and learning mindset within the organization is critical and it is worth investigating whether training budgets can be allocated toward coaching programs.

A learning mindset is not only a desire to get better, but also an acknowledgement that sometimes one does not have all the answers. We also often do not allow ourselves the space to truly isolate and unpack things. In day-to-day life, we are all going about our priorities and tasks carrying an abundance of challenges and issues around with us. Distractions and immediate calls on our attention are many and constant.

Many of us are therefore in the habit of acknowledging our challenges in only a fleeting way, while never truly addressing them, as we are pushing on with our daily lives. Although that can create some space for solutions to appear while the mind is not focusing directly on the issue, it equally does not allow us to isolate and unpack the challenge as an exercise using someone as sounding board, guide, and accountability partner.

Accountability in this context is all about accepting responsibility to find solutions for the identified and highlighted challenge, within a time-bound period, with a moment to review and learn, allowing for adoption of the lessons into the leader's ongoing approach.

What a coach relationship is really all about then is personal accountability and discipline. It is a discipline of carving out structured, dedicated, and uninterrupted time with another person to air, and describe the challenges being faced in a focused manner. The dialogue itself does not always have to be structured. At first, this can be an uncomfortable experience, precisely because there are no distractions. One has to be present and prepared to often talk about areas that we do not consider ourselves super comfortable or complete in. What is most illuminating though is that the answers generally all reside within yourself, when you allow yourself the opportunity to surface them.

Remember, the coach is not there to provide you with the answers. They will guide you to unpack and delve deeply into the issue and what you believe could be ways to move forward to tackle the situation. All angles and approaches can be analyzed, alongside use of tools and techniques that may help you to understand aspects of what is occurring at a human level. You can then better understand anything that is going on internally that is either helping or hindering you. These insights are golden and critical if you are keen to continue to develop as a people leader. No amount of formal training will be able to deliver the insights that ongoing coaching can. Understanding how you show up and what may be driving you emotionally is all part of honing your capabilities as a leader and as a communicator.

Consider now taking this approach into your day-to-day management. Often, it is felt that the leader has an incumbent duty to solve for all issues, as opposed to working to develop their team and enable them to be more successful. Try resisting the impulse to lay out directions or solutions and shift into a coaching mindset when circumstances allow. Ask your team open questions, what do you think we should do? What would be the impact of "x" approach? What alternative approaches can we action? Follow through and ask how individuals have found the passing of this responsibility to think critically and widely about the business, and how it has changed them in your one-to-ones and reviews.

The reason why investments into executive coaches are seen as holistic business investments is that if you level up your leaders and help them in turn to take a people-first coaching mentality into their business, the outcomes can be transformational in terms of culture, bottom-line business, talent acquisition, and retention.

Your External Network

LinkedIn is a such a powerful tool for curating and working with an extended network of executives and talent. Remember, that if you are reaching out to anyone in the network, to take the time to learn about them, and to thoroughly prepare. Respect their time also, always be succinct, to the point, compelling, and passionate in your outreach.

Do your research and identify why you would value the time of someone. Do not outstay your welcome or hassle people who may not engage on the platform as a matter of form and who, legitimately, might be super busy themselves. I have gained value from my extended network on a number of occasions including:

- Helping in hiring decisions.
- Deciding on career moves and job offers.
- Finding talent.
- Helping to learn or upskill in a particular area.
- Giving back by helping to introduce others to critical contacts for many of the same reasons as listed earlier.

HR Business Partner

The HR business partner can be a strong ally for the commercial leader for several reasons:

1. *Talent acquisition and development*: HR can assist in recruiting and developing a high-performing sales team, ensuring that the commercial leader has access to skilled and motivated individuals who align with the organization's goals.

2. *Performance management*: HR can help design and implement performance management systems (including commission schemes) that align with commercial goals, ensuring that individuals and teams are accountable and motivated to achieving targets. HR plays a key role in designing competitive compensation packages and benefits that motivate and retain top-performing sales professionals, aligning with the commercial leader's efforts to attract and retain talent.

3. *Training and development*: A skilled and well-trained sales team is crucial for commercial success. HR can work with the commercial leader to design and implement training programs that enhance the skills and knowledge of the sales force.

4. *Conflict resolution*: In the dynamic field of sales, conflicts may arise. HR can mediate and resolve conflicts, ensuring that the commercial team remains focused on achieving objectives without internal disruptions.

5. *Succession planning, diversity, and inclusion*: HR can work with the commercial leader to help keep a bench of talent at the ready and to promote diversity and inclusion within the sales team, fostering a broader range of perspectives and strategies for reaching diverse markets.

By collaborating closely with the HR business partner, a commercial leader can create an environment that attracts top talent, enhances employee engagement, and aligns HR strategies with commercial objectives, ultimately contributing to the overall success of the organization.

Marketing

For optimal outcomes, marketing and commercial leadership should foster open communication, shared goals, and collaborative strategies, ensuring a cohesive approach to market positioning, customer engagement, and the overall business success. An aligned relationship with your marketing leaders can help to enhance:

1. *Market research and insights*: Marketing can provide valuable market research and insights, helping the commercial leader make informed decisions about target audiences, customer needs, and competitive landscapes.

2. *Lead generation*: Depending on your industry and product, marketing can be an essential partner in terms of lead generation.
3. *Content creation*: Thought leadership, sales collateral, case studies, social media, name recognition, and event planning are all useful tools for the commercial leader to consider.

Well-Connected Headhunters

The best have a head to the ground in terms of the macro environment, trends in your industry, and, of course, in respect to talent availability and movement.

Extending the Culture of Coaching

We have touched already on the potential benefits of extending a coaching mentality into your business, to inform culture and to foster a creative, vibrant, performing team around you.

Numerous studies have explored the relationship between employee retention and various forms of investment by employers. These investments can take the form of training and development as well as wider programs geared at celebrating and growing the individual. If you as a leader are known for personally investing in and growing your people, this is a great way to gel your teams and keep your core together, while also defending your built culture.

Studies into this topic include:

- *Investing in People: Financial Impact of Human Resource Initiatives* (Fitz-enz 2001): Jac Fitz-enz explores the financial impact of various HR initiatives, including training and development and how these contribute to organizational success and retention.
- "The impact of employee benefits on the recruitment and retention of quality employees" (SHRM 2007): A report by the Society of Human Resource Management (SHRM) on the benefits of programs to attract and retain employees.

- "Employee engagement: the key to realizing competitive advantage" (Towers Perrin 2003): A comparative study to show that companies with employee growth investment policies retained and attracted better than those without.

Consider extending this initiative further by seeking to build an internal panel of mentorship across the business, which could be extended to identified talent within your organization. To do this, you must have taken time as an executive leadership group to identify potential leaders and people to develop across the organization. A group of potential mentees can then be matched to appropriate mentors across the business. Ensuring a culture of coaching is a sure-fire way to allow for a more open and fluid exchange of ideas to become commonplace.

Takeaways

- *Consider what is your starting point.*
- *Ask yourself what you need to learn in order to be better.*
- *Consider an executive coach.*
- *Ask how your company can support.*
- *Be a proactive user and servant to your extended networks, both within and external to your company.*
- *Support and grow a wider coaching culture within your company.*

CHAPTER 10

The CRM and Pipeline Management

Chapter Summary

- Customer relationship management (CRM) has to be the single source of truth; it is the data from which you will interpret, communicate, and base decisions on your business.
- The CRM will show you where you need to place your focuses, and will allow you to track your progress toward your goals.
- Consider your business' attributes when thinking about KPIs and metrics; use only those that add value and make sense.
- Reporting for the sake of reporting, helps no one; for clear insights to be gathered and put into action, get your reporting right, and then focus on creating outcomes for your business.

Back to the layering process on the pathway to creating your strategy! One of the priority tasks for any sales leader, whether promoted or embarking on a turnaround, or a new build, is to quickly establish the credibility and data-driven insights provided by the customer relationship management (CRM) system.

The CRM, and the data maintained within it, needs to be a trusted, up-to-date reflection of the trajectory of your sales operation. Not only will the data prove invaluable to you in discerning the trends, strengths, and weaknesses in your enterprise, but it will also allow you the capability of prioritization, as it will tell you the velocity of your business. You have to be able to rely on this tool, which means communicating its importance to the team.

Disciplined pipeline management and cadence are vital for any sales organization. This data is the lifeblood of your business and, for the sales leader, vital in terms of intimately knowing your numbers, as it will allow you to build your plans and business cases, execute against them, and monitor your progress.

It is a critical part of your communication and dialogue with senior management as well. If you cannot trust the data, you will not be able to forecast effectively or gain credibility in asking for support or investments. Therefore, always make the CRM a priority. Make sure that the team knows why you need this data to be on point, and message strongly that it is the responsibility of their position as customer experts to update and maintain all progress across the customer group.

It is not unusual for such reporting to be in a poor state when you first step into the role, and it is incredibly important that you set the expectation that the CRM be the one source of truth on all current deals. It is quite common, if there has not been a focus on the CRM previously, for the data to be poorly and infrequently maintained. You need to be able to rely on this data when speaking about and planning for your business. Whatever state the CRM is in, you must take some time to tease out the current data and pay attention to what it is showing you.

There are many great resources available which go into CRM management in greater depth. That is not my intention here. Once your data is reliable, there is so much you can do in terms of producing meaningful reports and dashboards that allow you to run your business. Initially, and for the purposes of this text, I will only aim to focus on the high-level immediate data needs you should look to address when you come into this role. We will also spend some time understanding what that data might be telling you in terms of the health and direction of the business you have joined.

Do also bear in mind that certain metrics and KPIs may or may not be important depending on your industry and the nature of your sales cycle. In my industries, for example, we are dealing with more consultative approaches and longer drawn out sales cycles, with many dependencies. As such, I am less focused on sales activity reports and dashboards focused on metrics such as the number of calls or meetings. In a faster-turnover business, these metrics can be very meaningful, so make sure the CRM is gathering those insights you will need to run the business you manage most effectively.

Personally, I only start to get interested in activity reports if I suspect there is a performance issue, either building up or evident with an individual or the wider team. Even then, my focus would be on whether the contacts that are happening are at the right levels of seniority at prospect customers, and in pursuit of the right type of deals. It could be that coaching or other tweaks in training can help to resolve a lack of performance, alongside short-term goal setting, or, in some more extreme cases, a performance management plan or even an exit from the company. If an exit is contemplated, then the data within the CRM is important to bring the topic up to the individual, to set meaningful remedial performance management goals, and to help manage those as part of a performance plan to tackle the issue at hand.

The point is that once you have settled the basics and have a reliable insight into the trajectory of your sales efforts, then you can add or layer other data points to help you understand and improve your results. For now, let's focus on some basics. Just make sure that the KPIs you select help you to drive the business and not the other way around.

What Is CRM?

CRM is the database or SAAS tool in which all customer information and deal data pertaining to those customers is maintained. Maintenance of this data is critical. I use the word maintenance deliberately as maintenance takes work after all. Maintenance needs to become a habit.

Thinking back to the analogy of the sales team as an engine, one cannot expect an engine to perpetually run without fuel and maintenance. The fuel in this case is the data within the CRM. Good, clean fuel helps the engine run smoothly with less bumps on the road. Think then of the CRM as the oil tanker to fuel your sales engine. It can tell you a great deal about the health and trajectory of your business and whether you are hunting in sustained or structured ways or not.

This last point is super crucial as quality fuel maintains and enhances your engine. The quality of that fuel is essentially how accurate and up to date the deal data is, and an analysis of that data in the form of a pipeline will soon tell you how much fuel your engine has, helping you to anticipate and plan for stutters or hopefully accelerations on your path to meeting your goals for the business. Maintenance is the discipline to keep this data updated and accurate. An unmaintained engine after all will become less efficient over time and more susceptible to breakdowns.

The aforementioned takes work to establish. People may not be used to disciplined regular administration around their work. It is important that you set out your expectations early on and explain how and why this data is going to help not only you in your work but also the individual as well. Drive your cadence meetings from the CRM and use it consistently to drive the focus. This is all about responsibility at the end of the day. You are conferring expertise for customers and their markets onto your team. If the data is not telling those stories accurately, then expertise is essentially missing.

Once your core data is secure, expand the capture of important information. Entering information that shows why deals are lost as much as why they are won, alongside financial deal metrics, helps in understanding how the market is meeting your product or service. Gathering all data will allow you to provide additional support and investment to the sales force to increase opportunity. You cannot do that if only successful data is entered or analyzed.

Creating a Sales Pipeline

Every sale is a journey and there should be clearly defined milestones to show how leads are progressing through the sales stages toward closure (we will speak more on this shortly). You can determine a great deal about your business by immediately understanding the number and size of your deals at various stages of the sales process.

Essential CRM Inputs

There is a great deal of data that can be stored in a CRM including e-mail and call details. Some minimum fundamentals you need to see are:

- *The customer name*
  o The client or prospect entity you are selling to.

- *Contacts*
  - o Who are the primary relationships in the deal and what are their titles and roles? It is important to map all of these contact points, especially in complex deals.
    - Consider what will happen in the event of a salesperson leaving your business. How easily can someone pick up the understanding of who the customer is and what roles each contact plays in your relationship?
- *Opportunity*
  - o Details and financials on the deal being worked.
  - o Alignment to the offered product should also be captured.
- *Revenue and profit*
  - o Total spend and profit metrics (gross or net profit, depending on your company's focus).
- *Deal stage*
  - o It is important to define how the deal is progressing through its stages; also, from a pipeline analysis point of view to define a percent to each stage. You should also take a note of the day counts in terms of how long deals are stuck at various points and then do some analysis as to the reasons behind the delays.
  - o Deals at an early stage should have small percentage conversion applied to them. A brand-new opportunity, for example, might be weighted to 5 percent and a qualified one to 20 percent. Once you have had a meeting and depending on your closure rates, perhaps this moves to 30 to 40 percent. A proposal takes the deal to 50 percent, and negotiation somewhere between 70 and 80 percent, a verbal acceptance of the deal 90 percent, and once the signed contracts are in, 100 percent. Depending on your industry, you could then have further milestones to include, such as compliance steps and implementation.
- *Weighted totals*
  - o You derive the weighted total of the deal by taking the deal amount × the percent as determined by where the deal is in the sales cycle.

- *Close date*
  - o Deal stage, weighted deal total, and close date now become important stage posts to be thinking about when judging what should be coming in during the period you are surveying, in forecast terms.
- *Win and loss information*
  - o Did a deal go to a competitor? If so, who? Is it stalled and, if so, why? Are we missing a feature? If so, how much is the dollar value of all current "lost" opportunities?
  - o Equally important is to gather the information as to why we won, so that case studies and internal learnings and training can become more widespread.
  - o Stalled or on hold means that the deal could come back at some point when the client or when your product is ready; ensure that visibility is maintained on these leads with a sense of when and how to resurrect these processes.
  - o Marketing—knowing where the lead came from is also critical for marketing; for example, it can help the investment case for events. Marketing also needs to be able to support spreading the word about your differentials in the marketplace, so information on why you were selected over competitive solutions is incredibly helpful. Ensure that when at events your lead capture goes into a "leads" resource on the CRM, whereby qualification and conversion to actual sales opportunities can be developed and tracked. This can help you judge your investment and which events you should be maintaining, or not, across your calendar year.
  - o Product—ensuring you make use of the data of missed opportunities due to missing features or nonexposures to markets, will help you in developing your roadmap priorities with your product function.
  - o Within any sales review, it is worth capturing what is working and what is not working. Ensure that you are not trying to solve for these elements at the time but do combine with the data you are gathering so that you can

more clearly determine what the opportunity loss is. You can then bring clearer narratives to other functions or senior leadership as needs be.

The Sales Journey Defined

Given in Figure 10.1 is an example of the milestones that a deal could progress through on the way to being won and revenue recognized. At a minimum, you would want to track each of the suggested stages, but other milestones could be valid to your business, such as know your customer or buyer (KYC/B) compliance or implementation steps, so be sure to incorporate those into your process if required.

This is all about considering when the cash actually shows up on your P&L. A signed deal often does not mean revenue until the customer has been fully implemented, or the product or service is delivered and payment made, so have a view on the next stages of the process until the money is actually recognized on your balance sheet. Quite often, it is necessary to combine your pipeline with a revenue forecast, which interprets when or how your deal will hit or ramp in the P&L, once you have signed it. Always focus in terms of pure revenue recognition.

The stages and percentages given below in Figure 10.1, are examples only, and you need to consider what makes sense for your business.

Stage Duration

You should also consider the time taken on average to close a deal and whether deals are being held up in any part of the cycle by tracking the day counts. It is easy to add to your reporting how many days a deal is held within each stage, to be able to get a sense of speed to revenue. This, in turn, can help you discern how many deals you need to have active in your pipeline to make your targets. Metrics like time from closure to onboarding/implementation and closure to spend can also be vital, depending on your business, as lags to revenue may be involved, which could be shortened once identified and addressed.

Again all this data can provide clear insights into areas for training or wider internal discussion with colleagues and departments in regard to

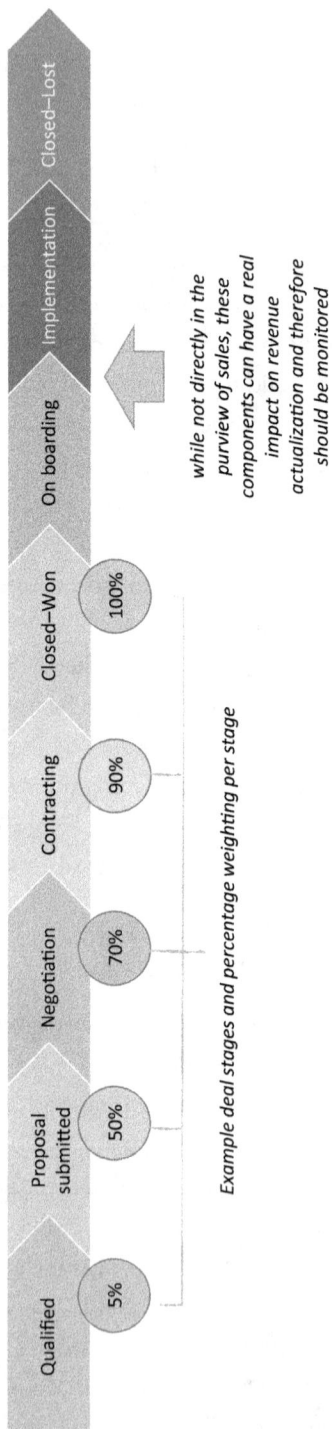

Figure 10.1 Weighed totals example

understanding how to make the sales process more efficient or the accel-
eration to revenue faster.

A Weighted View of the Pipeline

Having set up the aforementioned, you will be able to pull some insights
from your data. For example, the number of deals you have in each sales
stage and their total potential worth to your business if closed.

While it is good to see the total revenue potential of your pipeline,
this of course will not accurately tell you the full story. Focus now on creating a more accurate view of your pipeline's potential worth by factoring
in the maturity stage.

You will not win every deal and of course, each deal will be at a certain
stage of maturity and as such, they will drop onto your P&L at varying
points throughout the year. Hence, it is important to see the weighted
position. The weighted view of the pipeline is where you can ascribe a
percentage to each stage of the sales journey.

For example, you may have a new opportunity worth $1M in the
qualification stage. Would you want to report this at its full value? Imagine the attention this large deal will have if reported early as a certainty,
when you, in truth, have only just begun the sales journey. Of course,
it should be called out as a promising new prospect, but the value you
should report at this early stage should be reflective not only of the deal
potential but also of its maturity within the sales process.

If it is newly qualified, this is again great news, because you know you
have a real opportunity on your hands; however, qualification is only the
very beginning of the sales effort. As such, ascribing it a small percentage

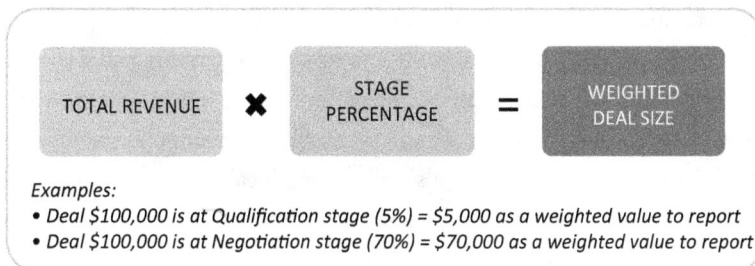

Examples:
• Deal $100,000 is at Qualification stage (5%) = $5,000 as a weighted value to report
• Deal $100,000 is at Negotiation stage (70%) = $70,000 as a weighted value to report

Figure 10.2 Weighed totals calculus

certainty of conversion of say 5 percent means that you only report this deal as worth $50K at this point, which is a more accurate representation of the deal when looking at or reporting the strength of the pipeline at this specific moment in time.

To be clear, this is not "sandbagging," which is the practice of overly conservatively valuing deals in the pipeline. This is about being able to better predict the financial flows coming into the business.

Conversion Rates

It now becomes important to understand what your deal conversion rate is but let us assume you win 50 percent of all deals. By the time you are formally presenting a quotation to your prospect, you would therefore assign a 50 percent weighting to deals at this stage and so on. This means you can predict with some certainty what the pipeline is worth right now to your business. The negotiation stage now means you are more than likely to win this deal. A verbal agreement from the customer or deal signature could be 90 percent and contract received, of course, 100 percent. Remember always, that a deal is never done until the signed contract is received.

Example of High-Level Reporting

Once you have these elements in place you can move onto reporting and pipeline analysis. It is easy to pull reporting from the CRM to help you spot trends and areas for immediate focus and attention. The first report you should consider is what I would call an "all opportunities, all stages, current year close dates, by salesperson" report. This can usually be easily configured in the reporting section of your CRM.

This report literally does what it says on the tin: grouping all deals by salesperson, by stage, including total and net revenue figures and includes all wins and losses. You can export to Excel and manipulate it to add weightings, and most CRMs also allow graphical representations and other data to be added to customize reports, minimizing the manual work to produce a meaningful statement.

The Figure 10.3 is an example of how the various sales stages could be used to start to interrogate the data in your CRM. Now the data is

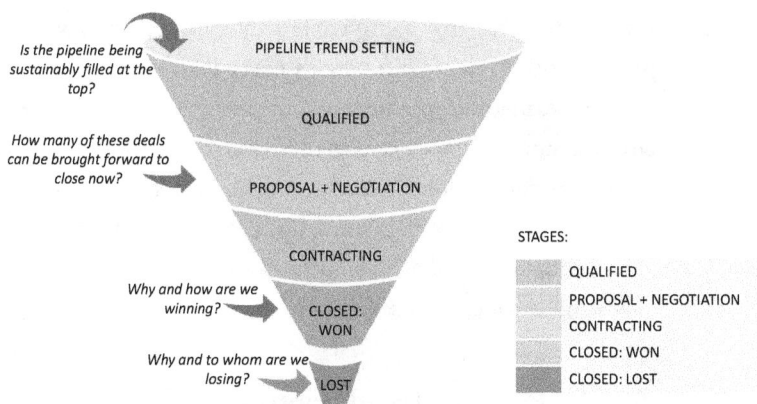

Figure 10.3 CRM *pipeline funnel analysis example*

working for you and allowing you to tell the stories of your current sales campaigns and their resonance in the market.

Pipeline Reporting Without Strategy Is Not a Recipe for Success

Once you have set it up, this data then becomes the staple for looking at and discussing the pipeline with your team in your cadence, in group meetings, or in your one-to-ones with the sales folks. Be cautious of becoming a mere "pipeline jockey" though—a manager who solely runs through the existing opportunities without actively focusing on under-standing the market, or advancing deals through support, improving the identification of new opportunities, and ensuring successful closures. Pipeline management in the absence of a clear sales strategy will not help you to maximize your team's potential in the market.

Ultimately, the CRM should be a step toward further development of your sales strategy. It tells you what is happening right now; it does not set direction. You, as the commercial leader, need to deploy your team's focuses best to maximize market wins. Once a strategy is in place, the CRM should help to indicate the progress being made to achieving those set goals. If you are running pipeline cadence in the absence of a clear go-to market strategy that can be understood and articulated by the entire team, then you are not maximizing your focus and chances of injecting real momentum into your sales engine.

Be curious. Understand how your people are creating their expertise and opportunity. Work to figure out how to make their lives easier and how to support increasing the aperture on your target markets and prospects. Velocity and momentum are important in sales. It is not enough to study reports and ask your people, "What support do you need?" Clearly, one should do this in support of one's team, but becoming attuned to the data and to your people, as well as to your markets, allows you to know what can potentially enhance your sales machine.

Pipeline Trend Spotting

In the simplified full pipeline snapshot representation in Figure 10.4 (not broken down by salesperson), you can immediately spot some trends;

- The good news is that there are a number of deals in the advanced stages; you should be banking on winning most, if not all, of these.
- The bad news is that the mid stages are weak; there are very few deals here comparatively, which is setting up a feast or famine trajectory.

	Total	Weighted	
Prospecting	$1,017,501	$101,750	
First meeting	$4,559,000	$1,367,700	
Quote	$59,000	$17,700	
Management presentation	$680,000	**$272,000**	
Proposal on market	$505,850	**$303,510**	$575,510
Totals	**$6,821,351**	**$2,062,660**	
Closed lost	$3,687,000		
Deals won YTD	**$354,273**	$303,510	$575, 510
Projected '17		**$657,783**	**$929,783**

Pipeline Comments
1. Need Mike's data in SFDC to get the full picture
2. Close dates need renewing/this is not an accurate picture; many deals past their projected close
3. Pipe strength should only be viewed in terms of 60% and above; in those terms, pipeline is weak at $303,510-$575,510 potential only
4. Our potential is in the first meeting stage—suggest we revisit and focus on ways to build strategic proposals to convert as many as possible
5. Suggest a full opportunities review as many are running to huge sales cycles (see highlights) and also to determine true close dates—how many of these deals are really still live?

Figure 10.4 Example insights from CRM data

In observing the aforementioned full pipeline snapshot, the priorities in terms of actions that you might potentially emphasize could be a combination of:

- Focus and finish—close out the outstanding deals as soon as possible, by bringing key deal closures forward.
- Focus to move first meeting prospects to quotation stage as a priority.
- Refresh the top of the pipe—quickly begin prospecting for new opportunities to fill the top of the pipe.
- Understand what the marketing mix is, to create greater or more opportunity:
  - Why is the team not focusing on this so much?
  - How do we find our opportunities currently?
- Understand why we are winning and losing:
  - Winning—build case studies, detail winning use cases, translate these to marketing, use all gathered insights for sales reviews and end-of-year learnings. A rigorous process here, will allow for the better identification of similar potential clients in the market.
  - Losing—learn to sell/win against the competition:
    - Better understanding of who the competition is and what you know about their propositions, strengths, and weaknesses compared to yours.
    - Production of competitor battle cards to enable better positioning in deals.
    - Highlighting potential training requirements for the team.
    - Identify where to invest to win; build or prioritize needed features.

First Steps in Analyzing Your CRM Data

Once you have good reporting in place, you can start to review your CRM data in detail and pull out some points for attention. Example questions to consider when reviewing your CRM data might be:

- How mature is your pipeline?
  - What proportion of your deals are at an advanced stage, that is, close to closing?

- How long is your average deal cycle?
  - o Knowing the average deal closure time and dependencies on this (KYB, compliance, onboarding, etc.) is vital to being able to predict your business.
- Are you running out of fuel?
  - o Momentum in sales is everything and if you are not as conscious of filling your pipeline at the top as you are on closing, then you will have a famine and feast on your hands; you are striving for a smooth journey, not a lurching bunny hop, to the finish line.
- What is your win–loss ratio?
  - o If you are winning less than 50 percent of your opportunities, you need to understand why and work to improve your conversions.
- Why are you wining/losing?
  - o This analysis allows you to find more repeatable business. Work internally to improve understanding of where and why you are losing to be able to promote mitigation strategies.
  - o This activity, in turn, allows you to then define winning use cases, which, can help you to become more targeted in your sales approaches.
- Where are your leads coming from?
  - o Knowing this allows you to consider your marketing mix and investments to help the top of the funnel.
- Is your team consistently contributing?
  - o Knowing the team and their businesses better allows you to consider training and support initiatives to improve where the deals are coming from.
- Where can you provide support to feed the pipeline?
  - o Investments could come in the form of marketing; thought leadership, event hosting or attendance, product enhancements, and so on.

You should also know how many deals were signed by each salesperson in the previous years to get a sense of what to target them on in your current year.

So why is all this so important? Sales leadership is about knowing your business such that you can interpret it for your leadership, see around corners and anticipate what you will need to make your goals. It is about authoring and leading your go-to market approach and supporting the identification and development of new enhancements and markets. Using the CRM, immediate themes and insights can be unearthed, that will allow you to mold your sales plan for the most immediate and best outcomes for your business.

CRM Principles

Ensure that the following principles are known early and upfront with all of your people:

1. The CRM is the true source of all prospect information.
2. It is the salesperson's responsibility to ensure that all customer contacts and opportunities are defined and up to date.
3. If it's not in the CRM, it doesn't exist:
   a. That is to say, if a deal is not in the CRM and shown to be progressing through the deal stages, it does not exist and commission cannot be paid on it.
4. Update your sales stage and sales close dates regularly and accurately:
   - The salespeople should be disciplined in updating close dates, which, of course, can move as deal dynamics change.
   - Close dates have to be as accurate as possible to allow you to report what revenue is likely to land and when.
5. Loss analytics:
   a. Ensure that you are capturing your loss data as well; it is important to know why you are losing deals so that you can pivot as required.

Takeaways

- *Attend to improving your CRM data as soon as possible.*
- *If a deal is not in the CRM, it does not exist.*
- *No record or deal progression, no commission.*

(*Continued*)

(Continued)

- *Deal stage and close dates must be maintained and accurate.*
- *Analyze and isolate the main topics the CRM data is telling you and formulate plans based on that data.*
- *Remember that CRM data and pipeline analysis in the absence of a go-to market strategy is not, ever, going to transform your business. The CRM is there to monitor your progress toward hitting your strategic goals, not the other way around.*
- *A salesperson should know their business:*
  - *Market/segment.*
  - *Clients/prospects.*
  - *How and why we win.*
  - *Where to hunt.*
  - *What is the winning value proposition?*
  - *Their numbers:*
    - *Month.*
    - *Quarter.*
    - *Year.*

CHAPTER 11

Create Your Culturally Aligned Sales Strategy: The "Cornerstone"

Chapter Summary

- In order to mesh strategy to culture, you will need a positioning statement to help align, focus, and identify the pillars of your detailed sales planning.
- The cornerstone tool will be used in communication to align and gain support as well as gather invaluably useful feedback from across the business.
- Keep it directional and high level; do not be tempted at this stage to head into details; these will come in your more detailed sales planning.

The cornerstone plan has been mentioned a few times now. Let's focus on what it is and on what it entails, specifically, how will it become a compass for building direction through followership toward a single cohesive plan. Additionally, we will explore the process of crafting it and the contexts in which it proves most beneficial.

At this point, you will now be well versed in what the goals of the business are. You will know your numbers and you will be keen to put in place plans to achieve them. Where to start? Creating a strategy and a sales plan can seem like daunting tasks when you are at the bottom of the mountain looking up, so think of the cornerstone as the first brick you are laying in the creation of those structural documents. The cornerstone is therefore the vision statement that will focus you and the business on the direction you are taking; it is your north star. It will tease out the core themes you have already identified. Later, you will build in the detail with your team on where to focus and how to win through the more functional sales or go-to market planning. This strategy document is about binding people on the why, the what, and the how.

So what is it exactly? Within the context of building your sales strategy, the cornerstone is essentially a one-page slide, a summary which distills everything about your business, the year's objectives, the how and the whys, where you will focus and what you will need asap to achieve all of this. As covered in the previous chapters, you will by now have gathered sufficient inputs and data sets on your enterprise, that will allow you to pull out and elevate some of the threads you have uncovered in your time in role so far. You will now develop them into a series of headline statements of where the focus needs to be. Go-to market strategy is all about creating and maintaining focuses: clarity of purpose, allocation of resources, understanding of, and playing to competitive advantages, all within the context of effective customer-obsessed execution, aimed at clearly defined winning use cases.

This is also a vital opportunity as part of beginning to cement in your cultural leadership. What we are looking for here is an easily shared, clear, communicable message, which you will use to accomplish a number of objectives covering both business goals and cultural aspects pertaining to your organizational ambition.

Business Goals

Business goal objectives you can cover using the cornerstone template will be as follows:

- Communication of the financial and business goals of the period in question, usually the current financial year.
- Communication of the pathway and vision in terms of what you seek to achieve in top line terms.
- Demonstration of how all will come together to win collectively by embodying and sharing values and behaviors to reach the goal.

- Communication of the key priorities and summary objectives that must be addressed.
- Setting out and sharing of your own focused objectives.
- Communication of what needs to be true to win.

Cultural Aspects

The cultural elements you can cover in the cornerstone would be:

- Gaining alignment and support from your senior management.
- Creation of an alignment tool to support collaboration across your fellow departmental leadership.
- Creation of a tool of general communication to kick off any internal sessions, such as; town halls, sales meetings, strategy sessions, offsites, or company days.
- To surface the topics in summary that you will build upon and detail for the executable sales plan.
- To use with individuals in discussion or with the full sales team.
- To use to onboard new joiners across the organization.

The goal is to articulate a simple aligning vision. We will accomplish this by weaving all the inputs and data you have harvested into a compelling, succinct statement, which provides the summary core headline elements only, in order to create a singular vision. It serves to focus all around you on the core objective of why and how you do what you do. It serves to ensure that everyone not only fully understands, but is as equally focused on the journey toward the set goal as you are.

Consider it to be the piece that meshes the culture to the mission. Once you have this, everything else becomes by degrees easier and your task of building a detailed sales plan becomes less daunting. I call this statement the cornerstone, because it is on this platform that you will build consensus and the foundations of your mission-aligned culture build.

The cornerstone is the first stone set in the construction of a masonry project. All other stones will be set in reference to this first stone. The cornerstone therefore sets the position and development of the entire structure.

The Cornerstone as Communication Tool

What we are looking for here is a tool that can be used to communicate throughout the business. The audience will be your leadership, your team, new joiners, and the functions and leaders around you. It could even possibly be used or adapted for a key account quarterly business review, as part of cultural alignment to your customer, to assist differentiation through forging partnership. I did this once myself with a customer whose financial rigor and people-first culture were very similar to my company's. Often a first step in moving from supplier status to genuine partnership is the realization that the buying and supplying company's missions and values are actually entwined.

The cornerstone is focused primarily on the financial year set out ahead of you. Longer term statements such as three- or five-year plans should be kept to summary statements; for example, you might choose to reference the target share price or turnover you are building toward over a longer piece. The point is, that if you do hint at this stage about the longer journey, say a five-year ambition, then just position this at this time. Think of the cornerstone as seeding the top priorities and focuses; as such, the vision of the longer journey is all that is needed for this document.

Try to make the statement intentful and accessible and write it with the sense that anyone in the organization should be able to pick it up, interpret it, and buy into it. Summary statements such as these have also become known as vision statements. Within a vision, you should be focusing on the why, the what, and the how of your business and its purpose at a high level. It is clearly aimed toward the outcomes you want for the business in sales and the financial goals you are set to achieve, but more than this, it is also about culture and the behaviors you want to elevate in order to meet your goals.

By putting emphasis on the values and expected behaviors, you are also showing that you care about the hows as much as you do about the whats. This already makes it a more holistic statement, as it is as much concerned about culture as it is about ambition. How you go about your business every day informs how you will achieve your numbers. You are already here signaling that you want the team to think differently about their businesses and how they act internally to efficiently win in the market. We pursue this approach because the most efficient and fun way to meet your ambitions is through doing it together. Furthermore, if united as *one* team coming together in a concerted effort to reach the finish line, you will essentially build a sustainable engine that can consistently propel you forward year on year.

The Cornerstone Plan Template

In the example shown in Figure 11.1, everything is boiled down. While it incorporates the summary of the sales and financial targets of the year, they are not its sole focus. Let us now explore the elements that comprise this directional document.

Simplicity

As this is intended as a high-level communication and discussion document, simplicity and conciseness is key. This vision is critical and while your business may be complex, the vision itself must be simple. Make everything clear and meaningful to the state of the business at the point at which you find it. Make it understandable for all; think of handing it to a new joiner; for example, could they grasp the key components, direction, and values of the business in a quick read? It should be the universal blueprint anyone could clearly digest and sign up to. It should succinctly tell anyone where you plan to go, how to plan to do it, and with which focuses. Remember, these focuses are likely to change as new opportunities or threats appear, it is important to understand that this should be a living document. Return to it often and update as needed as things evolve.

Begin With the Themes You Have Identified

Let's consider what you are likely to have gathered now in terms of data points related to the business:

- You will have met your people and be on the road to knowing them; you probably have a sense of who you have and what you might be missing in terms of skill sets or support.

YOUR LOGO

PLAN

2024 AMBITION | **20 NEW CLIENTS** | **LAND and EXPAND**
- Conversions to full rollout
- Upselling and Cross-sells

$ +25% Growth
- $1,800m TTV 2024
- $800m net profit 2024

VISION

To be recognized as the go-to enabler of flexible and mobile work arrangements globally, allowing for fast deployment of world class talent, seamless contractor engagement, smoother onboarding, timesheet to payroll and financing, while increasing efficiencies and misclassifications.

"The one stop global workplace enabler that makes you unstoppable."

STRATEGY

FOCUS AND FINISH | **WINNING TECHNOLOGY** | **THINK LIKE INVESTOR** | **INVEST IN OUR PEOPLE**
LAND AND EXPAND

- Define market and key opportunities
- Regional voice; technology accessibility and optionality as a competitive strength
- Focus on continually improving go-to market effectiveness in collaboration with adjacent functions
- Became a consistent employer of choice

- Laser focus on the deals that matter (new logo and existing customers)
- Understanding the localized support needed to deliver pilots and develop long-term coauthored projects
- Grow a superior product capability across our businesses
- Build an ability to develop, attract, motivate, and grow tomorrow's talent

- Revenue now
- Build pipeline to drive development and investment

Revenue at TBD % growth | Develop Customer Studies/Use Cases | Project Revenue | Land TTV Conversion to Vision with $1.8m TTV Segments

MISSION

- Lead from the front
  - Build and develop team
- Focus and finish (new business)
  - Define the use cases
  - Define the country markets
  - Prioritize the largest most profitable prospects and deals
- Land and expand (key accounts)
  - Develop strategic plans to penetrate and protect all strategic clients
- Understand the needs of customers and partners

BEHAVIORS

Inspire High Standards While Showing We Care
- People first
- Expect excellence

Build Bridges to Win
- Act across the business to win
  - Work across all functions
  - Be the voice of the region/market
- Grow smart

- **Shape Our Markets and Adapt to Rapid Change**
  - See around corners
  - Know the customer

- **Be a Talent Multiplier**
  - Grow self
  - Grow people
    - Identify and develop talent
  - Adopt individual personal development plans tied to annual review

VALUES

- We make it our own
- We make it better
- We succeed together
- We create magic!

PRIORITIES

➤ Meet/develop/build team
➤ Understand pipeline
  ➤ Transfer wins/oppos across regions
➤ Define the key oppos/priorities
➤ Focus activities to plan
➤ Build the use cases

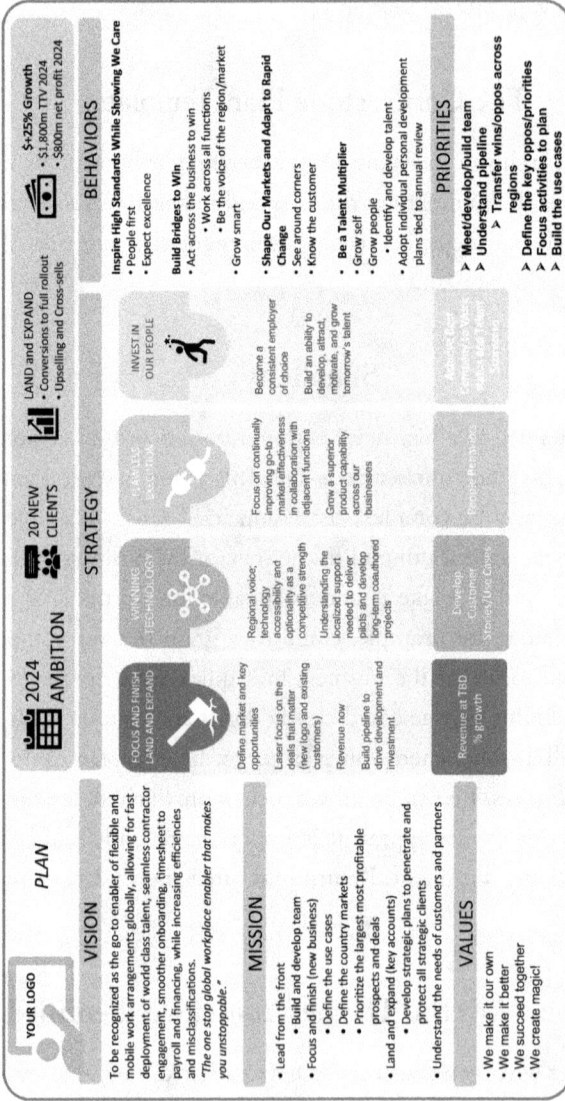

Figure 11.1 Cornerstone template

- You will have reviewed your CRM and pipeline data. This has likely given you a high-level sense of the challenges ahead and where you need to focus to make the most impact on a short-, medium-, and long-term basis.
- You will have surfaced trends in terms of what the CRM data is telling you. Where is the pressing need: filling the top of the pipe, converting on the mature deals, or ramping customers post contract win? Highlight these accordingly.
- You will have identified some key trends in the business, for example, velocity, capacity to find opportunity, profitability, customization versus standardization, speed of contracting, or compliance steps which need reviewing in order to increase efficiency.
- You have likely developed your internal network, collaborated with and understood the key focuses of fellow leaders and department heads.
- You have aligned with your senior leaders and executive sponsors in terms of their visions and perceptions of the business.
- You will have completed your enhanced SWOT and 90-day plans.

In building your cornerstone, settle on a few of the priorities and the themes that encapsulate those elements which appear most pressing to resolve or focus on, in order to make immediate impact. This is of course a template that I would encourage you to adapt and make your own. Let's now break this document down in detail.

Financials

We are in commerce. We must know and begin with our financials, always. Know your numbers. Know your targets and the financial language of your business. Placing these up front and center on your plan is indicative of what the whole team is there to deliver. The culture is the how. The numbers are the why and everyone on the team has to know this north star and how their contribution adds up to the directional total. A cultural shift is to have everyone, even cross-functional areas, thinking creatively in terms of how their business affects the overall business.

These figures will be specific to your company, industry, and product, encompassing elements like sales revenue, volume, or gross/net profit, either individually or in combination. They may involve objectives such as aiming for an Initial Public Offering (IPO), within a set timeframe or having a target share price. Additionally, there might be a specified three- or five-year trajectory with articulated ambitions regarding the business' scale. Regardless of the metrics, prioritizing them and consistently communicating them through the foundational one pager will guarantee that everyone remains sharply focused on these pivotal goals, which are the ultimate directions of your journey.

Vision

This should be no more than one or two sentences. Think of it as your cocktail party elevator pitch. It should be easy to understand and should be compelling. Examples might be:

> *We want to be recognized as the global leader of delivering transformational value for the customers of the world's largest digital brands.*
> *We remove inefficiencies and stickiness by enabling global supply chains to transact faster, unlocking value into the buyer–supplier relationship.*

Consider what this statement is designed to do. Imagine you have stepped into the lift with the managing director of the most singularly important prospect on your pipeline and she asks you, "what does your company do?" You have at best 10 seconds, so find a compelling way to summarize the essence of why you are in the business of what you do.

Here, I would encourage you to look at the work of Simon Sinek and his book, *Start With Why*, and ensure your statement focuses solely on the why of what you do, not the how or the what. Think of it this way: you want to be compelling enough to get to the next question from this MD. "How do we find out more?"

Mission

This is where you can start to communicate your themes. In the cornerstone example shown earlier, we are setting an agenda of personal responsibility in:

- *Focusing and finishing*—executing on the must-win deals.
- *Landing and expanding*—getting the maximum squeeze of juice out of the strategic customers while defending the existing customer relationships.
- *Customer obsession*—Becoming more customer obsessed and customer centric around language, approaches, and understanding—customer and people first in combination.

Values

As important as what you do is how you do it. Your company may already have a stated set of values. If not, and especially if you are in a turnaround situation or a new build, it is your opportunity to start to speak about the values you want to see lived through the way your teams go about their business both internally and externally. In the example earlier, we are focusing on:

- Personal ownership and responsibility.
- An open culture of working together—building bridges to win.
- Being creative, "creating magic."

Others might include:

- Integrity.
- Innovation.
- Giving back.
- Self-growth and learning.

We will explore exercises later on that can aid you in recognizing your own personal values and personal brand. This process can provide you with insights into behaviors and values essential for building your desired culture.

Incentivizing the Right Behaviors

Once you have built and aligned your cornerstone, it is important to put elements into action straightaway. As previously discussed, cultural values and behaviors are useless on the page without them being demonstrated and incentivized.

Remember, you are likely changing the status quo whether you are newly promoted or in a turnaround. As for a new start, you are setting the path. In all cases, once you have the buy-in of senior management, my first port of call to put things into action, would be to speak to your HR business partner.

Incentives, awards, and annual and half-yearly reviews are all important stage posts in the people year of any organization. Ensure that you set targets, rewards, and emphasis on your set and agreed values and behaviors through the people side of the business. Having recruited HR to also drive these focuses through your business, you must also live and demonstrate the values and behaviors yourself. This may require coaching moments with the team to help break set behaviors.

For example, instead of providing solutions and direction to raised issues, ask your people what they think they should do. Encourage them to go and speak to other functions and to use their internal networks to find solutions for themselves before presenting a case for decision. In the case of needing to pivot or drive more opportunity in the market, again, ask the salesperson what they need in order to unlock things, and where they feel they should be focusing. Both practices are signaling that you are expecting your colleagues be thinking creatively about their markets.

Further to this, ask yourself: Does the commission or bonus culture support the values and themes you have set out? Does the annual review process tie back to these themes, values, and behaviors? Can the reward mix, including spot rewards or quarterly and annual company award recognition, support you better? Consider the structure of your offsites and quarterly sales review meetings and ensure that there is a segment for companywide recognition of behaviors in action. If this begins to involve other functions, then so much the better.

Putting a Name to the Themes

Having identified some of the key themes and challenges that you will need to address in your strategic plan, it is time to focus on those and give them a name. For that to resonate and land strongly, you will need to give names to the core elements in a way that centers the collective thinking on the journey. This helps in the creation of a narrative and a focus to which you can bind your people and organization. The aim is to ignite the imaginations of both your teammates and the broader organization, aligning them with your vision for the business.

Critical to formulating a culture is to set a direction and a path that all can buy into. Let's unpack that a little; to buy into something heart and soul, the person needs to be able to agree to the current state, visualize the proposed outcome, and believe that the steps and focuses outlined will get us there, together. If that is in place, the person can take that next step in seeing how their role and contributions will support that success. Descriptors that get to the core essence of the issue are important therefore to help capture the imaginations of the audience.

Summarizing key elements into short, sharp, compelling, and understandable categories will help to accomplish this, help you convey the message on priorities, and help when creating your short- and long-term plans and communications. Boil things down to their essence. Do not overexplain or complicate at this point. Also, be mindful that in a business where a lot needs to be addressed, you should really only focus toward four or five achievable outcomes. Any more than this confuses the issue, and rather than narrowing the diameter of focus to ensure delivery, it can guarantee that folks will try to accomplish everything and, in so doing, achieve nothing.

Recognize that this is a living document and an evolving process, so if you put some focus actions down fast, so much the better; move the complete items into your achievements pile and adapt your plan toward the next objectives. This is again about motivation, belief, and prioritization. It is easier to sign up to, and believe you can accomplish and go after 3 to 4 targets, than 5 to 10.

As there could be multiple topics, ask yourself: Is your focus new business, development of key strategic accounts, profitability, restructuring the overall effort for efficiencies in the sales process, or a mixture of them all? Can some of these points be grouped together under these topics? Now, consider what is your overarching theme or themes that will tie all of this together.

A reminder: do not be concerned about the how and the whys of the topics just yet in terms of solutions. Of course, our impulse is to jump into solving for challenges, but remain high level for now. Jumping in to solutions without structure will only over time lead to a sense of a leadership that is not grounded, or in control of what it is doing. Be wary of this because for those outside of the leadership team, the impression can be very demoralizing, even if the messages from leadership are confident and strong. The longer there is a disconnect, the more likely you will face talent leakage as team members decide that the objectives are not measurable or realizable.

Further to this, also consider the current company culture. If there is a founder-centric environment, or if all discussion of the priorities and focuses remains only at the board level, then the rest of company can feel isolated and unsure what the direction is. The cornerstone is again about communicating and laying the path in an inclusive manner. That's what builds buy-in and culture; top down does not build trust, belief, or loyalty. Let's consider some examples of how to do this; this is not meant to be an exhaustive list but hopefully something that gives you some ideas. Examples might include:

- Coffee and cocktails.
- Focus and finish.
- Land and expand.
- Simplify to win.
- Win it together.
- Make it better together.

Let's dig into some of these deeper.

Coffee and Cocktails

This may not fit all businesses; it does depend on what your offering is, but those which have a complex sale and the requirement to build value propositions may value this as a theme. Does your company have a prospecting issue? Do you know your customers sufficiently? Is revenue being left on the table because there is no concerted key account sales plan or strategy? Coffee and cocktails as a theme is about building vital connection. This is all about getting out there, spending quality time in front of clients and prospects through making new or deeper connections.

How best to do this? By getting face-to-face and getting to know these folks more deeply. All the customer activities in mapping out the key decision makers, buying processes, identification of opportunity, competitive analysis, and share of wallet, whether new or existing, can all be gathered under the title of "coffee and cocktails." Just as you have built the connection authentically with your people within your business, so your company must do the same with your customers. In simpler terms, making the most of the valuable moments with the customer, regardless of the setting, leading to a deeper grasp of their priorities and plans. It is also about helping to secure valuable insights on how you can collaboratively achieve mutually beneficial outcomes through your offerings.

This terminology can also be used if you're needing to generate new opportunities in a concerted way. Maybe, for example, the top of the pipeline is looking thin compared to the number of deals that are in mature stages. Focusing the team on coffee and cocktails is one way to ensure good client interaction is happening consistently.

Focus and Finish

Are a number of deals stuck at advanced stages? Are there onboarding complexities to do with compliance or technical implementation? Is speed to revenue an issue? Is the velocity of sales not delivering with the urgency required? While a new business strategy could also be encompassed under the title "focus and finish," this can also simply be used to impart ambitious focus across the group pointed toward a number of defined initiatives.

Simply put, focus and finish means getting stuff done with laser focus. You can point this toward the most mature deals in your pipeline and put singular focus on what needs to get done to close these off asap. For example, imagine identifying the potentially transformational deals on your pipeline and placing this emphasis on advancing them as quickly as can be at the start of your financial year.

This is not designed to be a singular activity eclipsing all others, but to drill down to what needs to be true or what needs to be done in order to make certain deals drop sooner. Executive engagement, process fixes, and investment are all a part of identifying the keys to unlock the deal. The finish element of "focus and finish" would be the identification of your top three targets and a laser focus on completing all activities to advance these buying candidates through the sales process to final signature, implementation, and onboarding. All of this can be tied back to ambition and momentum. Nothing is more exciting than showing the team and company exponential growth featuring how you achieved it, including where you are going to go next. This statement entails installing a focused commitment on the growth plans, specifically translating that commitment into tangible results through decisive action.

Focus could also mean the identification of your key use cases, the buying customer profiles combined with a targeted approach to prospects, markets, and geographies. The pressure of hitting numbers can often lead to a shotgun approach to new business, essentially shooting for everything. This often happens when salespeople are under enormous pressure. If you have done some existing customer analysis, to understand whether the deals being won make sense or are actually profitable for you, maybe this is showing that a structured approach of winning the business you want to win is not actually in place at the current time.

An exercise to go along with the "focus and finish" theme could be to ask your team what are the top three things on their lists of to dos and what would be the meaningful impact on the business in terms of revenue or efficiency gain if they were to eliminate these tasks now. Have them identify these, publish them, and narrow their focus onto these activities with a timeframe for completion. Then, do not forget to review these regularly. Bear in mind, some could be worth recognition and celebration when eventually put down.

If your product or offering is less consultatively driven, then mini competitions around lead generation can also be considered and your language can adapt accordingly. These environments are usually about sustaining positive energy, matched to focused activity. Ensure your learnings about good practice and winning approaches are combined with instilled competitiveness, matched to rewards and the frequent celebration of success.

Alternatively, you may be in a matured position where you have all the component parts you need and it's just about focus and execution now. You have a settled team, you have connectivity to support functions, you are not distracted by firefighting. You know how to sell, what to sell, and where to sell. Now, it's just all about momentum. It's about kicking forward in a new business sense. This would then be about anchoring to the ambition, pushing to the next horizon, and connecting a team toward this new objective and ambition. This can be underpinned by a competitive analysis or market feedback that shows you how you are able to win, thereby placing a focus toward maximizing the velocity of realizable gains.

Land and Expand

We will focus on key account and relationship management, within a later chapter. For now, let us be clear; relationship management is all about sales. It is about so much more than simply protecting and serving the existing client and about ensuring expansion as well. It's about partnership and aligned goals and values. If your key account or relationship management function is not carrying financial growth targets, you should change this asap. Within this context, it is important to differentiate between new business and existing account business sales plans. Both are about identifying opportunity and building pipeline potential, but relationship management is also about the analysis of key relationships in the account, share of wallet, threats, risk of competition, as well as executing against possible expansion opportunities.

Questions to ask yourself in relation to how you currently engage with your existing customer base would be:

- Does 80 percent of your revenue or volume come from only 20 percent of your customer base?
- Are you considered a supplier or a partner to your key strategic customers?

- What is the product mix you have sold to your clients? Are cross-sales, or is global expansion of deals possible?
- What share of wallet do you have compared to your competitors?
- Has relationship management been kept separate from sales or is it a neglected function?
- Have you a hero client helping you to launch a new offering?
- Have you learnt and shared the lessons of this customer sufficiently internally, so that other prospects and opportunities might also be discovered and closed?

Landing within this context means getting the deal across the line and into relationship management. It can also mean landing the elements of the expansion pipeline the team has identified. Expanding means the creation of a strategic sales plan to identify and access the full delivery potential of that client, whether locally, regionally, or globally.

To get to this point, you need to understand your customer mix and where you are in identifying and servicing all that is out there. If it has not already been done, you should analyze your existing customers by whatever metric makes sense for your business. It is not unusual for you to find plenty of opportunity that has been left on the table, through an exercise such as this.

Frequently, an existing customer review will throw up the fact that the majority source of your company's revenue or profits are generated using the 80/20 rule. I have been at many organizations where this is true. In such environments, you will find that the few, the 20 percent, provide the majority of the company's income and revenue. This is clearly a massive risk to the portfolio, should you lose anyone in the 20 percentile range. But, you should also look at how to grow that segment.

Ensure as well that you do not neglect the 80 percent remaining. These clients should be analyzed to understand if any could be promoted to key accounts with focus and attention. The remainder, or "long tail," should then be segmented and viewed in terms of whether the effort and cost to support them makes sense. Many companies are now moving to banded support environments based on revenue or volume such as platinum, gold, silver, and bronze. Again, it's about ensuring that your focuses are advancing your cause.

Simplify to Win

Is your sales effort messy? Is the sales team trying to go for any or all opportunity? Has your deal analysis shown that certain deals or customers are better or more profitable than others? Is your deal cycle or onboarding too complex? Does it take too long to get to revenue post signature?

In these circumstances, it is better to focus the sales team and company on the use cases that make the most sense related to where you are winning in the market. Narrow the focus down to defined use cases and hone the pitch approach and marketing messages toward these. Follow up with a structured approach to defining additional targets in the market.

This effort could also be in finding ways to streamline your internal processes. Here, you need to map out all the stage posts following contract signature and before the client generates volume or revenue for your company. Are any steps taking too long? Do things get significantly held up and how does this affect revenue and forecast reporting? Having identified the issues, brainstorm or approach your fellow functional leaders to find solutions to the problems.

Win It Together

What level of collaboration do you see in the pursuit of winning customers? Is the expertise in your company fully utilized to help build the value propositions to win? Are support presenting opportunities, if spotted, to sales? Are all customer-focused functions aligned and operating smoothly together? Win it together is about that creation of *one* team working in harmony, together to win. Remember to also celebrate together.

Make It Better Together

Similar to the earlier point, but more focused on adaptation, removing unnecessary steps and hurdles. Think of this as the group finding creative ways to help your customers come on board faster and with maximum effect. This is about instilling a sense that good ideas can and should come from anywhere in the company.

Strategy

This would be the main pillar of your approach to market. These would be very specific to your business and its maturity. Ensure you are picking core themes that are clear and relevant.

Behaviors

What are the behaviors that underpin and create the values you have previously stated? Be as clear and practical as possible. If you have these already published in the company, then reinforce those.

Priorities

List here at a high level where your focus is going to be. What are you seeking to accomplish, and where will your personal focus and finish laser be directed? Also consider what help you need.

Pulling It All Together

This document is all about the culture you are building and the followership you will create around the pursuit of *one* aligned plan. The plan can pivot, the goals and approaches can change, but the why, the ambition, and the values that will get you there are constant. Reinforce these through consistent communication and leadership through example.

Takeaways

- *Setting the vision is the first step to alignment of, then building of followership, and your culture bonded to your direction of travel.*
- *Use the cornerstone in all of your internal communications, to your leaders, to your cross-functional colleagues, and to your team and new joiners.*
- *Use the cornerstone to tee off offsites and company days.*

- *Reference and iterate as needed, so all are clear and aligned on the mission.*
- *Use to identify the topics you will deep dive into, using your detailed sales planning.*

CHAPTER 12

The Power of Hospitality, Offsites, and Company Days

Chapter Summary

- Breaking day-to-day dynamics can be a powerful tool in building stronger appreciation and connectivity across the business.
- Use hospitality, offsites, and company days to fast track your cultural build.
- Utilize events and activities as opportunities to generate ideas and enhancements that can be incorporated into your go-to market strategy, customer development, and efforts to improve process efficiency.
- Consider the power of "incremental gains" on your business.

Hospitality: the basic function of spending quality time, of eating and drinking together, is about fundamental human connection.

Whether it be a coffee, drinks, or a dinner, it is a moment to connect and understand someone at a deeper level. It is to me the essence of humanity. Eating and drinking together is an act of generosity conveying on others that you respect and value them enough to share meaningful time with them. These are the moments when we can forge bonds, align, and, sometimes, when required, tackle difficult challenges or topics.

Hospitality in business is often primarily associated with relationship building with customers. Absolutely, this is a critical element. However, as a business leader, it is a fundamental tool for building closer ties with your team and thereby forging culture. It is also a tool that can be focused on individuals, subsets of the team, or the entire organization for different goals and outcomes. Any group that enjoys the company of each other, that is ambitious, curious, and fun is more likely to stick together.

Authentic leadership is about getting to know your people, creating, if you will, a family. The fundamentals of this are to tie all together on the single goal and journey. Families of course do not always have to be harmonious and in agreement. Tension, conflict, and alternative points of view are very important to a fresh, dynamic, healthy, and diverse group. The authentic leader will encourage people to be their true selves, by ensuring that there is a safe and nonjudgmental environment in which people can perform highly, while being respected and treated the same as everyone else.

Hospitality is also an opportunity to change location and therefore the dynamic. People relax and share more outside of the formal work setting or one-to-one meeting. To be clear, this is not meant to pry on your people and one does need to respect boundaries, but knowing and taking an interest in people's lives, helps you to understand how they are showing up at work. It can also assist you in knowing when you may need to help them to be the best that they can be. Teams that bond on several levels and beyond purely work topics tend to gel and stick together. Encouraging and participating in knowing your people outside of a pure work context is an important facet of this.

Some people are of course more protective of their personal lives than others and this is also ok. That does not preclude you from having a coffee or a beer with them. These are times when you can share your values and focuses as a person, which are likely to enhance the values you want to see in your organization and dynamics.

When you get the team outside of work, you can also create groups that may not normally combine regularly or as closely as you would like. For example, I have been in organizations where customer services, sales, and product all acted like independent fiefdoms. I would always be shocked to see this; after all, all these functions operate in the support of the customer. It is also always interesting to find companies running so fast day to day, that they lose sight of where and how they are winning. Getting these folks offsite and together is a first step in helping them to forge bonds and to realize that they too have challenges and goals that are shared. Offsite exercises like brainstorming also benefit hugely from multiple perspectives garnered from a diverse team's inputs.

The Power of the Offsite

Huge leaps in culture can be made through well-curated offsites or internal company days. This is especially the case if you need to reset a tone or find ways to pivot from a current strategy or path.

Getting everyone out of the office, or at least out of the daily routine, and into a new space can focus minds and spark creativity, especially if the team is actively involved in presenting their businesses and in brainstorming activities related to the business. A new energy can be fostered by deliberately arranging for folks to head out of their comfort zones by introducing themselves to people they have not met. "Clumping" at company events can be the dynamic of seeing colleagues constantly hanging out with their day-to-day relationships. Even consider seating arrangements that put sales, operations, product, finance, legal, compliance, HR, marketing, and so on together, table by table, as an exercise in breaking down these barriers.

People bonds can be forged and strengthened if the event is also fun. Themed events, even fancy dress or agendas developed and led by rotating functions, can all serve to add a dimension of enjoyment to a corporate gathering. Be mindful that dry, discordant, or noninteractive events can have the complete opposite effect than intended. Nothing is worse than confirmation that you work in a challenging and dysfunctional environment. Nothing is more demotivating than witnessing a room descending into endless debate, away from the headline topics, without palpable outcomes, or to be a part of sessions without impact or purpose.

Tensions or disassociation can appear if people or functions are allowed to exist seemingly separately from one another. Tying back to basics such as a P&L focus, sales performance, customer obsession, or use cases, can usually bring a consistent viewpoint back to sessions. Having a strong thematic through-point is important to bonding diverse groups and functions together. Once you have it, consider using the cornerstone at the top and perhaps even the tail of the meeting, to reinforce and remind what we all gathered to do each day on our mission. Remember to celebrate as well. Once the hard work of the day is done, celebrate the meeting, your colleague's achievements, and market wins before kicking off a social element or activity.

If you are seeing an element of dysfunction in the meeting, for example, because of a lack of product features or market focus, then these points should be called out and captured in a structured understanding of what is at stake. This could be, for example, description of the issue, the impact in terms of volume, dollars, or sales, specific customer impacts, or lost opportunity. Capture these items and keep the agenda and positivity on track by placing them in an actionable parking lot, with ascribed responsible colleagues named with the mission to come together to develop potential solutions. Ensure always there is clear time-bound action and follow through setup, especially if there are deeper issues at play. Consider ongoing forums where progress updates on these projects can be shared to ensure momentum and focus.

Offsites can also be specifically for subset groups, such as sales or simply the leadership cohort. If as part of your enhanced SWOT analysis, you have identified the need to build bridges to win across functional areas, for example, then offsites can be the environment where real breakthroughs are achieved. Consider, for example, a gathering of all functional leaders where your cornerstone plan is communicated and discussed, followed by exercises in aligning other leader's priorities and goals to the commercial path. The final cement in this cultural build could be personality or psychometric learning based on assessments. These tools can help the group to collectively understand their leadership styles, preferences, and strengths, as part of finding improved ways to come together as a cohort. If you are considering using psychometric or personality tests, widely recognized examples include the following:

- *Myers-Briggs Type Indicator (MBTI)*: A popular personality assessment that categorizes individuals into 16 personality types based on four series of opposites: extraversion versus introversion, sensing versus intuition, thinking versus feeling, and judging versus perceiving. It can provide insights into communication styles, decision-making processes, and team dynamics.
- *Hermann Whole Brain Thinking*: Associated with the Hermann Brain Dominance Instrument (HBDI,) is a

methodology designed to help individuals and organizations understand and leverage the diversity of thinking preferences in problem solving, communication, and decision making.

- *DiSC Assessment*: DiSC stands for Dominance, Influence, Steadiness, and Conscientiousness. It helps individuals understand their behavioral preferences in the workplace. This can be particularly useful for team building and communication strategies.
- *Leadership Circle Profile*: This 360 degree assessment combines feedback from self-assessment and input from colleagues to provide insights into an individual's leadership competencies and the underlying assumptions that drive behavior. It's often used for leadership development and coaching.
- *FIRO-B (Fundamental Interpersonal Relations Orientation— Behavior)*: This assessment explores interpersonal needs in the dimensions of: inclusion, control and affection. Understanding these can lead to better communication and collaboration across teams.

This is not a comprehensive list. Work with your HR and leadership to identify the specific goals of your gathering, as well as the context of how the results will be used. When considering the format of your offsite, also consider using a third-party practitioner or facilitator to help to ensure the assessments are both administered correctly and interpreted effectively.

Activities and Events to Consider

The offsite or company day is a real opportunity to maximize the potential of having companywide and diverse groups together and focused. Consider the following activities and events and how they might help reset or kick start a culture build:

- *Communication*—for example communicating the cornerstone, new direction, sales plans. When considering individuals, certain events could be enhanced by taking quarterly check-ins or end-of-year reviews offsite.

- *Learning*—leadership-style review and exercises, forging better ways to work together.
- *Department-led agendas*—sessions led by specific departments or functions; "get to know finance," for example.
- *Cross-functional brainstorming events*—events geared at determining how to improve the go-to market and how to land and expand clients, as examples.
- Understanding existing customers and how and why we win opportunities, including sharing of approaches to further develop these.
- Market and competitive analysis.
- Exercises and games to learn more about each other and their passions.
- Coaching and mentorship sessions.
- Awards and celebration of milestones and recognition of key contributors or performance, married to values and behaviors.

The Power of Cross-Functional Brainstorming to Find Incremental Gains

Having the opportunity to gain access to a diverse set of backgrounds and experiences in the pursuit of improvements is a precious thing. Make sure you harness this. Not only will it help to improve aspects of your business, but it will support your efforts in the creation of the optimal sharing and collaborative culture.

Set the task of breaking into teams with representation from across the business units, with focused topics to consider and find solutions for. It could be accessing new markets, improving onboarding processes and times, and anything that could move the needle on your business.

This is of course a team sport, and good ideas can come from anywhere or from any department. They are equally valid from finance as they are from operations, sales, or customer support. Capture the inputs and review with a view to moving the company forward through either incremental or sizable changes.

Do make sure that these insights and ideas are not lost. Ensure that time-bound actions are assigned to the implementation of ideas. Ensure that progress is reported on and updated across the organization. Reward ideas that have had significant impacts on the business.

Incremental Gains

Incremental or marginal gains refer to the process of making gradual and continuous improvements in a company's operations, processes, or culture over time. These improvements are typically small in scale but, when accumulated, lead to significant overall progress and positive outcomes.

A prominent example from the sporting world came from the world of cycling, through the efforts of Sir Dave Brailsford, a British cycling coach. His approach as performance director for British cycling was based on the idea that making small, incremental improvements in multiple aspects of cycling could lead to significant overall gains.

Brailsford's approach yielded remarkable results. Under his leadership, British cycling achieved unprecedented success in the Olympics. Team Sky, whom he also represented, won multiple Tour de France titles. Initiatives and improvements do not need to be revolutionary or seismic to make a significant impact.

Incorporate and structure this approach during your offsite and company reviews and you will ignite and strengthen a culture centered around the sharing and fostering of creative ideas to enhance your business. Consider in this the many potentially positive impacts this approach can have on your business and on your corporate culture.

Business Benefits

1. *Efficiency*: Incremental gains in identifying and eliminating inefficiency from production, supply chain, customer service, or onboarding.
2. *Productivity*: Focusing on productivity enhancements and task management to improve without disrupting existing operations. This could be CRM or marketing tool improvements.
3. *Customer experience*: Seeking regular feedback through customer events, day-to-day interactions or quarterly business reviews (QBRs)

can result in higher customer retention and positive word of mouth in the market.

4. *Innovation*: Encouraging employees to contribute innovative ideas and make small changes to products or services can foster a culture of innovation, leading to increased competitiveness.

Cultural Benefits

1. *Employee engagement*: Incremental gains in employee engagement on issues affecting morale can lead to a more committed and engaged workforce.

2. *Communication*: By consistently improving communication channels and practices you can enhance transparency and strengthen trust among team members.

3. *Diversity and inclusion*: Incremental gains can help to foster a more inclusive workplace by addressing biases and improving hiring and your overall culture.

4. *Well-being*: Small improvements can lead to healthier and happier employees with the effects of increased focus and loyalty.

5. *Leadership development*: Investing in the ongoing development of leadership, skills and qualities can lead to the development of more effective and empathetic leaders.

6. *Collaboration*: Encouraging cross-functional collaboration can result in better teamwork, idea sharing, and problem solving.

7. *Recognition*: Recognizing and celebrating all contributions and achievements on the path to building and maintaining your culture can further reinforce cultural build while boosting morale through demonstrated appreciation.

In both cultural and company improvement, recognize that significant change often arises from the cumulative impact of small and consistent efforts over time. By encouraging employees at all levels to contribute ideas for continuous improvement, organizations can achieve sustainable progress and adapt to changing circumstances more effectively. As Brailsford explained, "the 1 percent margin for improvement in everything you do" is the seed to unlocking the creative potential of your group.

Takeaways

- *Use the power of hospitality at an individual, group, and company level.*
- *Authentically get to know your people and encourage the same in the group.*
- *Use fun, interactive offsites to communicate, brainstorm, bond, collaborate, and deepen cross-functional ties as well as to celebrate wins.*

CHAPTER 13

Create Your Sales Plan: The Living Document

Chapter Summary

- Good news flash! Your cornerstone will have already identified the main pillars for your focused sales planning.
- Work with your team to bring their market plans into a structured approach that meets your targets and objectives for the year.
- Review, adapt, and pivot as needed. Good plans are flexible.

Let's start with some good news. The good news is that if you have already created your cornerstone slide, you should already have the essence of your sales plan down in high-level summary. Now, it is time to get some meat on those bones and time to ensure that your go-to market team is clear on where to prospect, how to win, and what to deliver.

The Budget

Your starting point is always the budget. Understanding where your numbers are coming from is about understanding your organization and leadership. The experience here will vary dramatically from company to company. I have been in companies where the sales leader is expected to produce the year's budgetary targets and I have been at many more where the target is handed down from finance or senior management, often, particularly in the latter case, with no inputs or collaboration from outside!

In one organization, it was arbitrarily declared that a 100 percent growth target was required based on no more than this was what was expected of a company at this stage of its growth cycle. Nothing was developed beyond this top-level ambition. Clearly, if the job of budgeting is siloed and not encompassing all facets of the go-to market team, this can make the job of the commercial leader exceptionally challenging. A combination of bottom up and top down makes the job of planning, motivating, and executing much easier.

This is why the new year can be so daunting within a sales group, especially if the top-down approach is experienced. The inexperienced sales manager or sales person for that matter is often confronted at the beginning of every new financial year with the exercise of totally resetting. They start again and stare in shock and awe at the massive number put before them to achieve. From this perspective, the mountain seems exceedingly high indeed. This is why the old sales adage of "how to eat an elephant" sticks. Essentially, the lesson here is not to be shocked into inertia or to launch into unstructured shotgun like shooting for everything, but to break the target down and "eat" the massive beast in small measures.

When looking for the building blocks to your new financial year, the pipeline should hopefully show you some deals and activities you can begin to count on with some degree of certainty. Deals that were started or not able to be closed in the last calendar year are the immediate building blocks. Adding to this, your existing customer spend or sales expectations of spend growth, can further give you a sense of how the year will be constructed. Now, you can gain a sense of what the gap looks like.

Then, it's about identifying where to focus to fill the gaps and even succeed on a stretch ambition. When considering this aspect, it is fundamental to have a sense of each of your salesperson's businesses and all the tools at your disposal including marketing budgets, preplanned marketing initiatives, customer events, product launches, and other potential contributors to your prospecting.

You should also seek to identify your "must-wins" and the sense of the activities that need to be prioritized in order to secure these. Here, I would be looking to identify the real needle-movers: those deals large and strategic enough that landing them early would do a great deal to establishing momentum and reducing the overall target. These should feed immediately into your "focus and finish" message. Bring whatever resources you can to taking down early the big targets in this respect.

I would also advocate, if at all possible, for beginning the budgetary planning process within the third or last quarter of the previous year, as anything later can effectively mean it is Q2 before you know it. Again, I have been at too many places where the process begins on day one of the new financial year or where sales kickoffs happen in February or March. I have even worked for a company where additional sales kickoffs were required in July, as things were not travelling to plan or organized effectively earlier. None of this helps the morale or direction of the go-to market team.

In my opinion, the later you start, the sooner you are planning to fail. Companies that only deliver the new year targets around the time of a sales kickoff in Q1 always shock me. In large part, a quarter disappears within the blink of an eye before a proper strategy for the year is considered. This is why Q3/Q4 is vital not only to your current year, but also to the planning for success of your next financial year.

Asking for Individual Sales Plans

Something I started doing early in my sales management career was to ask for each member of the team to produce their own sales plan or summary of approach before the budgetary process would begin. I would do this by setting a deadline and by asking for their plan on where and how they would focus for next year, including what number they felt would be possible to achieve.

This does not have to be either a difficult or an exhaustive task that entirely consumes their focus. All in all, the ask would be for no more than two to three summary slides to encapsulate each individual's plan. One slide would be the ask to capture the key components of the year ahead in budgetary terms, breaking down what the building blocks would be. I would then ask for a slide, or two at maximum, on the opportunities and risks and any asks they might have of the business to ensure all this could happen successfully. These asks could be that training and investment in marketing or events or entertainment were made available.

Focus and Numbers	O's and R's
Plan / Accounts / Targets	Topic
• $	Narrative
	Key Initiatives
	Topic
	Narrative

What we need to win?
1. Topic 1

Figure 13.1 Sales person plan template

Against these asks, there had to be a justification or return in terms of quantifiable sales or outcomes expected.

To accomplish this more easily and allow them more time to consider their plan, I would give the team a simple template to help focus their inputs and make it easier for me to compile and review. I highly recommend doing this to save you a lot of time later, especially if you are going to compile the inputs to produce a deck detailing the plan. If you ask for folks to create plans-free form, you will receive back all manner of presentations which will vary wildly based on the PowerPoint skills of the individuals. Using a suggested template will only save you time in the long run and will help you to create a flowing narrative and structure.

Example individual new business sales plan template is shown in Figure 13.1.

Existing Customer Account Sales Plans

For those focusing on existing customer accounts, there needs to be an additional input—a simple spreadsheet with spend by month and net revenue for the previous financial year by customer, containing a projection for the coming financial year. This projection should factor a volume start point from January 1. This input would give me a sense of the planned development of accounts throughout the year. I would ask this to accompany the sales plan templates for these team members.

Seasonal spend, if relevant, should also be factored. Clearly, these might also come with key account strategic plans, templates for which can be found in Chapter 15.

The Benefits of Building From the Ground Up

Why should you also consider doing this?

1. It is a great insight into how each individual thinks about their business.
2. It is a great way to spot potential coaching or training needs.
3. It would provide an insight into where people would focus their time and energies.
4. Weaknesses in the plan, combined with lack of focus, can easily be identified.
5. Mitigation or gap-filling planning can be executed earlier than otherwise might be the case.
6. You can judge just how conservative your team is—all salespeople like to sandbag their numbers a little!
7. When combined with the CRM reporting outputs, a sense check of the business can be made.
8. It would provide a basis for a strategy session once the inevitably higher target set by finance arrived and would allow for GAP analysis planning to take place, as well as enhancing brainstorming sessions on filling gaps.
9. Buy in. If one of the basis points is coming from their own data and experienced insights, then even if a stretch is added, there is a confidence the salesperson can garner from the overall plan.
10. Engagement—if you are deriving your numbers from the sales team, that by extension means that they are engaged in the process. It also means they are conferring their expertise and opinions of what they think is possible within their markets, sectors, or geographies.

Let's revisit once more the analogy of the sales team as a high-performance engine. I think we can agree that each component of a high-performance car is essentially expert in what it does. The same thing should be true of a sales team. As a sales leader, I expect every sales person to "know their business."

Of course in scale (matched to their expertise), each "component" of the business may be bigger or smaller than another, but they all add up and are vital to the whole. As a subject matter expert, (SME), any new business sales person should know their business as well as any key account manager working with a key account producing 80 percent of your revenue and profits.

What does "knowing your business" entail?

- Knowing your quota or target.
- Knowing your month, your quarter, your year, in terms of the numbers and run rate.
- Knowing the attributes of your target customers.
- Knowing where you will focus to get your numbers.
- Knowing your competition.
- Knowing the value proposition you will pitch to your clients.
- Knowing or having a sense of how to pivot if/when things do not go to plan.
- Knowing what assistance you need from the company/leadership to make your numbers.

The Sales Planning Session

This process is by degrees easier when you have already compiled the templates that each of your salespeople has provided. Why? Because they were the authors; as such, they have bought into a plan already. Now, you need to match that against whatever additional number have been set for you and work together to plug the gaps. This is where the "team" really comes into force. Either way now, all the collective heads are working together toward the goal of formulating the plan of attack.

Having created your cornerstone one pager and stitched the sales team and "gap" plan together, you will now have a plan that your team buys into that is married to your overall cornerstone plan objectives, that you can communicate to your fellow leaders in the business, and that you can use as the living document throughout the year. This is now what you can track your progress against.

The Rules of the Plan

1. The first rule of the plan is that the plan will likely change.
2. The plan is a living document; adapt it and update it as things change or new priorities become apparent.
3. Use the plan to review your results at the end of each month and at the beginning and end of each quarter with your team.
4. Come Q3 you know what to do—the previous year's plan is again your template for the next year and so on.

Takeaways

- *Have each of your team members deliver their draft plans ahead of budget time.*
- *Amalgamate and match to the sales target.*
- *Perform a gap analysis review and adapt your plan to figure out how you will fill any revenue holes.*
- *Review the plan each quarter in terms of how are you tracking, whether you need to pivot, and what investments you may need to win.*
- *Use deep-dive quarterly reviews to look back and to look forward with a critical view to your progress on the year.*

CHAPTER 14

Going a Step Deeper

Chapter Summary

- In this chapter, we will examine some additional elements you may want to address next, which can all help to take your approach to the next level.

The Language and Numbers of Your Business

Know your numbers and know your language. As a sales leader, you must learn to cut out the noise and focus on the fundamentals of your business. Depending on the maturity of your organization, product offerings, and approach to market, there will likely be a lot of competing attention for your time. Often, you are required to simplify and elevate the core components of your message; as such, you need to know the language you are using.

The key language you should focus on is the language that underpins the fundamentals of your business, and each organization holds certain metrics aloft. It is key to identify and understand those to be able to narrate your business in the context of these metrics.

Example Metrics

- Volume or total transactional volume (TTV)
- Total addressable market (TAM)
- Gross Revenue
- Net Revenue
- EBITDA

The list goes on. Identify your internal language, simplify your messages, and focus on the important numbers that drive you forward.

Having the Numbers Close to Hand

I would always write up the key messages, goals, and numbers on a white board in the office. I would also keep a back page of my notebook for the same when on the road. This was not only for me and my reference when on calls with management and colleagues, so that I might have immediate recall with fast reference to the key numbers or metrics, but also so the folks in the office would see what I was focusing on.

As I developed things, the super summary on the whiteboard would speak to broad goals beyond the current year, such as the projected size of the business in three- to five-years' time. An additional benefit to having such data visible in the office was to also connect the team to the journey through another reference, beyond the current financial year. Anyone in the office could see these numbers and it would often become a talking point.

I would be wary of doing this if you are bringing structure to an environment which has been more chaotic traditionally. Once you have shown structured growth, then it is a strong message people can believe in when you show a three- to five-year vision. People must buy into what has got you here, before they can absorb a plan of what will get you there after all.

When done at an appropriate time, it is about further instilling ambition and confidence in the group. I have been at several organizations where we have impacted the business quickly and shown dramatic improvements across all manner of metrics. Reminding folks of these achievements helps all believe that the next set of ambitions are equally achievable. It widens the aperture of the ambition and instills real pride and satisfaction in those seeing the milestones ticked off.

At first and without context, such goals can seem remote but when the team begins to believe, it is incredibly powerful. Remind them of how they initially felt when you mapped out the path and remind them of the achievements they have made on the way. Once you instill this belief, there is little you cannot achieve together.

When considering a culture, it is good that people feel connected to a larger mission than the current financial year in isolation. This again is a strong component to binding your people culturally to the mission. It is a layering effect. The cornerstone, the sales plan, the numbers visible in the office—all these provide a consistent reference for the group. Over time, the effect you will see is that your team will believe in the longer term mission and goals. They will also want to stay for it.

Deal and Existing Customer Analysis

When seeking areas to delve into more deeply, consider the following topics, if you have not already done so:

- A review of current pipeline and recent deals.
- Size, profitability, and/or revenue delivery of these deals.
- Makeup of the existing customer base.
- Where current revenue is coming from.
- Which deals are most profitable.
- How are current focuses enabling the identification and execution against similar prime use case targets in the market?
- Who are the whales? The strategic key accounts.

Deal Profitability

Not all customers or deals make sense. As it takes usually as much time to win a small deal as it does a large one, identify which deals are the best for your P&L and focus the activity on these. To do this, you need to consider how the sales team is applying themselves to the market opportunity. Where are the leads coming from, how are they being prospected, and if your offering serves multiple customer types, is there a more structured approach to identifying and selling to target customers?

Development of Use Cases

Always drive toward a more focused approach to identifying good customers. This approach will ensure a sustained pipeline build. It may

Define the challenge	• Describe the customer with 3–4 characteristics
What is the impact on the customer's business?	• Describe the loss of opportunity to the client
What is our value proposition?	• Describe the return on investment for the client, What is the elevator pitch?
How do we replicate?	• Describe the market, industry, similar companies, and geographies and create a bullet point plan of attack

Once you have identified your use cases, then one can broaden out the research to include who and what your competition is allowing for

Who is our competition?	• Describe the competitors, their value prepositions, and how we win against them
What are the prospecting approaches?	• Describe the message and activity mix to build a focused pipeline

Figure 14.1 A step deeper

take time to rewire current approaches, though the effort will pay dividends in the long run.

Once you have outlined your use cases, you can work on developing the customer list that might fit them and then work on the value propositions your salespeople should be taking into the market. Getting the team to think holistically and creatively about their and the business is about widening the diameters of their creative thinking. Developing use case-based approaches to market is about focusing that aperture and ensuring that their time and efforts are targeted for the maximum outcome.

Use the template shown in Figure 14.1 above to help to define your use cases and positioning against the competition. Once you have completed the exercise, publish and share each use case widely within the business and on your website.

Setting a Customer-Focused Offsite Exercise

Ensuring that your team knows its use cases and can describe your solutions in a customer's language sometimes requires a complete remodeling of the approach your sales teams are currently taking to market. It is by its nature a more consultative approach and requires a focus on the value dynamics of what is being sold. To achieve this, you have to get folks away from reliance on pure presentation and discussion of your services in your language toward the client. The shift is to be able to develop the value proposition through strong questioning married to an approach in the customer's language, conveying the benefits in cost savings, elimination of inefficiencies, and impact on profit or cost centers. All this has to be done in ways that are specific to the customer's situations.

Offsites or group gatherings can help you to begin to bed down and develop these use cases. On offsites, split your groups into cross-functional teams and have them work on each set of questions you have identified to build your use cases. Having a diverse multidisciplined team on the job can be a real asset to the brainstorming around these topics. Once they have developed these, take them to a role-play session to hone the delivery. Use the group feedback and learning to interrogate how the team reacts to this methodology and then set their goal to investigating what companies in prospecting terms might fit each use case.

Make sure to direct the final segment of the exercise toward exploring strategies to secure these deals. Discuss the proposed activities and messaging mix aimed at the prospect client lists that the team has cultivated. This step is crucial for instilling a sense of action and commitment to the new approaches. You could even sign off the activity with a committed action plan from each group who in turn can hold each other responsible in a competitive way, aiming for a prize or bonus based on developed results. Remember, unless these approaches are lived, they will never bed down.

Once you have compiled all the inputs and data and reviewed these, ensure that you build monitored action plans with time and date commitments to make sure that the momentum is maintained. Also, use your CRM pipeline review huddles to show, monitor, and drive the outcomes of the initiative. Just as with your team build and culture change, this will be a transition that you will need to monitor and reinforce until things become second nature.

Using Your Data-Driven Approach to Calm Chaos Through Direction

Some companies struggle because they have not fully built or defined their product offering or identified the use cases they are trying to solve for in the market. You may see the symptoms of this in the following ways:

- Chaotic sales meetings.
- Leadership or general meetings which focus on or dissolve into the minutia of the product, losing sight of what is working or, more often, not working, in the market:
  o Focusing on the minute details usually means that the go-to market is confused and ill defined, potentially even misunderstood.
  o This is turn usually means that the value proposition is not well defined and the reasons for not winning are not well articulated internally.
- Pipeline calls that are not giving the impression of a planned, sustainable growth toward annual goals:
  o The sense of team members gunning for any and all deals without a sense of planned purpose around targeting and qualification.
  o The real prospect that many deals won do not scale or ramp following implementation and the charging of initial implementation fees.
- Pipeline jockey meetings:
  o A focus in sales interactions with management only on what is there on the pipe, not what should or could be there:
    - This is a sure sign of focusing only on what is visible.
    - Shows a complete absence of strategy.
    - An absence of where to play and how to focus in the market—that is, where is the transformational customer acquisition strategy, is it broken down, or are large target clients identified by name only, with salespeople left to their own devices in terms of acquiring this business?

Have you ever sat in management or leadership meetings where the agenda quickly dissolves into chaos, usually involving intense discussion on detailed elements of a product or feature? Do these discussions usually end with no conclusion, action, or outcome, giving the sense that they are more of a battle of expertise than an exercise in building focus? Are there particular agents of chaos in your business who manage to deflect structured agendas and meetings in this way on a regular basis?

Chaos Grenades

I can recall being in a weekly management meeting where this battle of expertise would happen almost every time. The agenda would always end up hijacked and the time allocated would end with no resolution on any of the topics discussed. From a review of sales and customers, before you knew it, everyone would be pulled into a discussion on a legal matter or some element of how the product should be used in certain scenarios.

I have also been in organizations where certain senior leaders can act frankly like chaos grenades, helping to blow up any structure or process in a meeting. Ever witnessed an inexperienced salesperson ruin a perfect open question because they cannot handle silence? A good example was a founder who in a sales review asked the killer question which deserved a full understanding: "Why are we not winning or seeing more of this type of customer on the pipeline?" However, every time this occurred, another descent into the reasons why deals could not be constructed would end with this leader leaving the discussion entirely. Nothing would be captured for further analysis and each time, there would be no follow-through or resolution.

Meetings like this, which dissolve into opinionated, often passionate discussion which would run the clock out until the meeting dissolved with all going back to their daily focuses with no conclusions or actions to speak of, are highly demotivating. Repeated instances of this can also be very demoralizing as the focus tends to trend toward the negative and not focus on positive data-driven actions or any positives that might be at play within the organization. The corridor and coffee talk afterwards always trends toward how dysfunctional things are and further away from finding data-driven insights or conclusions. The worst outcome can then be that your talent will be focusing on finding ways out of your business as opposed to working to affect positive change.

The worst scenario here is when the management decides that the problem lies with the sales teams and that they are all rubbish and cannot sell. Yes, there may well be weak performers, but if the whole unit is failing substantially against the ambition, then something else is frankly at play.

Perhaps, it also reflects an incomplete product set against the competition as well. Data and clear identification of issues are your friend in these situations and your deep-dive early on in creating your data points, cornerstone, and more detailed sales plans will help to surface what you need to in order to navigate any circumstance, allowing for a more positive resetting of the agenda.

The solution is in finding your current winning use cases and to focus attention on these. This combined with finding ways to repeat good business, whilst highlighting any areas of weakness and quantifying the cost of these in lost opportunity terms, is the way to put organizational emphasis on getting you the help you need. Managing difficult and forceful personalities will always be a challenge; however, data and insight can cut through to establish structure. This is one of the key roles of commercial leadership. It is without doubt the duty of the commercial leader to help identify use cases that can focus everyone toward finding more of that repeatable, winnable, and executable business. It can also ensure a more comprehensive, focused message of what you do goes into the market.

Win–loss analysis will also help here to identify what is working or not working, which again helps to refocus the leadership dialogue. Bringing this to the table with a matrix of where your product is working and where it is not, with associated business cases, will help to prioritize and shift the focus away from the minutia. The sooner the conversation switches to what needs to be true to win, the better and more positive the management dialogues will be, leading in turn to more clarity on objectives and monitoring. Bringing your team closely into this effort to interpret the realities of the market for your business, in order to create clarity and define prioritization, will also have strong impacts on morale, purpose, and mission.

Be conscious as well that when it comes to unclear reporting lines, whoever owns the P&L should have the greatest say, but that sometimes things can get unwieldy at organizations, particularly as they mature. Be strong on this point if you need to be. Commercial leaders should take ownership of the market and possess the ability to interpret its dynamics for the benefit of the business.

Working With Marketing

In supporting your requirement to define buying personas, use cases, and client narratives that support your product or service, you have a friend in marketing. They are as equally focused as you are in a mission to identify and message the successes of your business, with the goal of bringing more opportunity into the commercial operation.

Make sure you take time to align with marketing on your goals and approaches to the market. Help them to understand the competitive landscape and what you need to support the team in the field. Such support could include:

- Targeted account marketing and lead creation using online tools.
- Content-driven lead creation—thought leadership, articles, blogs, and interviews.
- Exhibitions and events to drive lead generation.
- Customer-focused events—where new initiatives, feedback, and wider relationships can be messaged, gained, and acquired.
- Speaking opportunities and press engagements.

Combining with marketing to set a company exercise to bring structure and growth to the organization can be a real winner. They can also take key messages from the exercise into the thought leadership efforts they are curating, to help position your company well to be recognized as the leader in your space.

Understanding Your Competition and Creation of Battlecards

As you develop your sense of where you are winning and developing your use cases, you should also analyze why and to whom you are losing. As part of any deal qualification, you should also be aware of whom you are competing against. Battlecards are about gathering key intelligence to help your team and new joiners quickly get up to speed on how to sell against the competition.

Make sure win–loss analysis is captured in the CRM and discussed and reviewed frequently, so that you can see what trends or missing product features are at play in the market. Ensure you are also listening to the feedback from your customers regarding the same. Perhaps, training and development can help to improve your win ratios. It could also be that the compiled loss analysis helps you to build business cases to prioritize a particular functionality or access to a particular market.

Regardless of how high your win ratio is, it is also important to fact find on your competition, bearing in mind that this is likely to vary from geography to geography. Define the global, regional, and local players in the market. Once you have them identified, begin to better understand their propositions, commercials, strengths, weaknesses, and approaches, so that you might better compete against them. Bear in mind that you may also want to recruit from these players. Battlecards should be centralized, reviewed, maintained, and made easily accessible companywide. When considering a battlecard, ensure you are capturing the following information:

- Competitor overview.
- Where and how they play.
- Functionality.
- Their claims and how to address these.
- Their strengths and how to address these.
- Weaknesses and how to address these.
- Commercials—pricing and other data.

Bear in mind that some of this data may be captured through your wins as well as your losses. For example, when celebrating a competitive win, understand fully what drove the client to come to you as opposed to the rival.

Example Competitor Battlecard Template

Use the template below in Figure 14.2, to create battle cards for all your major competitors in each market you serve. Ensure that you make space in your quarterly or annual reviews to ensure that the team works through these, and takes these learnings into their marketplace dialogues with prospects and customers.

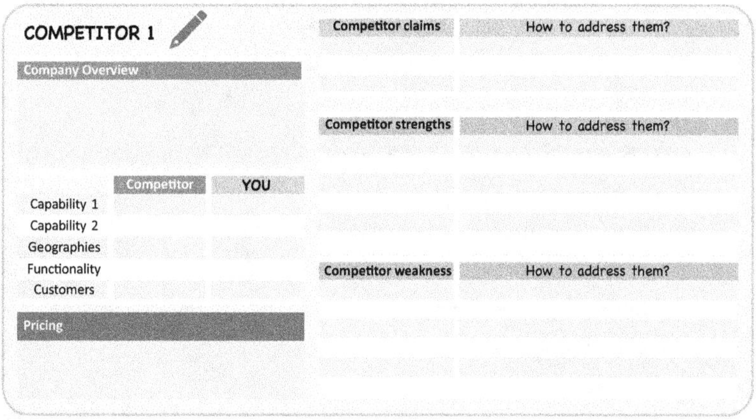

Figure 14.2 Battlecard template

Working With HR Business Partners

Having a strong HR business partner is a real blessing and can be a strong ally in training and culture build. Ensure that you align and work with them to support you in reinforcing and developing your team, behaviors, and culture. Ways that the HR business partner can support you are:

- Culture build through developing companywide values and behaviors.
- Helping you access training budgets for executive coaching and other training.
- Helping to instill a company coaching and mentorship program.
- Helping to install a process of defining and discussing identified talents within the organization.
- Aligning half-yearly and annual review processes and KPIs tied to values, behaviors, and actions.
- Training enhancements, including supporting programs, to strengthen your use case-driven approaches to market with value-selling techniques.
- Development of offsite and in-company meeting, messaging, and agendas.
- Spot bonuses and award schemes based on revenue, customer, and behavioral successes.

Takeaways

- *When you have set your cornerstone and plans in motion, carve out the time for deeper analysis on your business and its performance.*
- *Consider approaches to hone your go-to market approaches for better outcomes.*
- *Work with your allies in the business to continuously refresh and embed your approaches.*

CHAPTER 15

The Existing Client Review

Chapter Summary

- The existing and key account customer base requires its own set of approaches and sales planning.
- Changing embedded approaches can be challenging. This chapter will look at alternative approaches and templates that can help you gather the data that you need to pivot from transactional account management toward full land and expand planning.

As we have covered in earlier sections, existing customers can often be an untapped, underdeveloped source of revenue and so taken for granted. Just as you would research your market segment or geography, focus industries, and target prospects, you should also know your large and strategic customers intimately and build specific plans around them.

It can be surprising though, even in terms of companies who place structure and ownership around existing customers, (such as key account managers, relationship teams, or otherwise), how transactional those interactions can be. A lack of defined and implemented account strategy is to invite risk into your revenue stream as well as to lose potentially easier won opportunities.

It is far easier to sell to someone who knows and trusts you to deliver, than to someone who has not had the opportunity to previously experience your product or service. You should also know so much more about these existing customers than you would of a brand new prospect. As a new sales leader coming into role, it is well worth setting aside some time to develop analysis into the existing customer base.

Discover where the revenue mix is coming from, with what products and geographies. Look at the deal profitability and identify who the hero customers are and why. Determine how well penetrated the customer's C-suite is and observe who and what the account touchpoints are into your organization, as well as how frequently these interactions happen. Are your senior executives involved in any way and what of the experts in your organization? Is there a role they are playing to deepen the partnership you have already forged?

Find what reporting is in place and which forums are used to bring to life issues and opportunities at those clients. Are there account plans and pipelines and how integrated are they into the overall budget and sales plan? Finally, how are these successes translating into the marketing mix to find other similar clients? Is the client referenceable and could they, do they, participate in any customer gatherings or online sessions that you might host? Are they actively providing feedback to your organization and, if so, who is listening?

As we have repeatedly touched on, it is not unusual at all to find the 80/20 rule in full effect when it comes to an existing customer base, unless you are selling a standard off-the-shelf product within a set of defined support models. If you are in a company where 80 percent of existing revenue is coming from 20 percent of the customer base, this is an environment which demands attention; consider the risk of losing any of these accounts. I can guarantee that would put a dent below the waterline of any three- to five-year aspirational growth plan, if suddenly all the oxygen is taken out of the room by the need to backfill a huge revenue loss. While considering the risk, do also consider how replicable these accounts might be. Can they be described and can similar companies be found either in the same industry or within other geographies that you serve?

Key Account Risk

- A loss of one or two of these accounts could be seismic. If you are a global company, you are likely to have two to three whale accounts per region. Sales is always about growth and if you suddenly have to find ways to fill a hole and grow, you are in big trouble.

- Never take a key account for granted; just as they are important to you, you may be certain that your competition has also set their targets on acquiring some or all of your revenue. Consider where and how you might be attacked.
- Set to work to define your share of wallet and focus on expanding this through mapping out the client's C-suite, geographical presence, and affiliates or sister business units, including the opportunities housed in each.

Key Account Defense

- Consider how well you know your client. How deep and broad are your account relationships? Are your companies aligned on culture, strategy, and common goals? Companies who understand each other culturally and who are aligned on win–win initiatives thrive.
- Ask yourself what is the value proposition you are offering your client, how well do they recognize it, and are you just a supplier to them or considered to be a critical partner?
- Are your executives involved and sponsoring the relationship and account?
- What are the highlights, threats, and opportunities. Do you share the account with competition? Who are your competitors? What are the battlegrounds you must win to maintain the customer?
- Where and what are the expansion opportunities? Are they geographically independent in decision making or centralized?

Key Account Expansion

- Who owns the account internally? What is their sales style? Are they open and collaborative or tightly holding on to touchpoints or access to the client? Can they work to manage and coordinate a local, regional, and global approach to the client?
- What is the footprint of your customer? Can you expand by region or geography to other business units? Are there sister

companies or subsidiaries who might also use your product or service?

- Is the customer centralized or geographic in terms of how buying decisions are made? Do colleagues in other countries have access to client's executives and buying cohorts under a cohesive joined-up relationship management structure? Are you global acting locally or siloed in your approaches?

Who Are Similar Prospects?

- What can you learn from your current whale customers to enable you to find similar ones in the market? Will your customer endorse you to help you tell the story at their competitors or similar looking prospects?

Who Else Can Be Developed to Be the Next Whale Accounts?

- Who in the customer base from the 80 percent tail could be developed further? What is your definition of a whale, key or strategic account, or standard customer? Which customers can be promoted to the next revenue status level and what does this mean and look like?
- When planning your budget, how much of your budgetary target can be met by enhancing your sales efforts toward your existing customer base?

Bowties Versus Diamonds

When reviewing your key account strategy, think about how you are organized to protect and serve these vital assets to your business. Consider the account structures you currently have in place to face off to your whale and key account customers. Assess who "owns" the account and who is controlling the access and day-to-day conversations. The structure is very important specifically when thinking about a genuinely strategic whale account which you want to defend, expand, open up, and maximize. A traditional "bowtie" account management structure is not going to help you to maximize your opportunities to develop your account. Let us consider why.

The Bowtie Approach to Key Account Management

The bowtie approach to account relationship management is what I would call a traditional approach, whereby there is one owner of the relationship toward the customer. In this model, however, there is a major disadvantage in that the single owner is in effect a gatekeeper toward the rest of their organization. It is inherently risky. Similarly, the interface into only one main customer contact is limiting, as it prevents access to and learning about other elements of the customer's business. If I see this in play, I would expect that the nature of the relationship toward the customer is most likely transactional. If you do witness this, observe what the quality and depth of the interactions are. Consider how deep your penetration of the customer is in terms of key stakeholder relationships. Look at the asks of you from that customer. What plans and approaches is the account owner undertaking and planning? How developed are these?

The bowtie approach to account relationship management is shown in Figure 15.1.

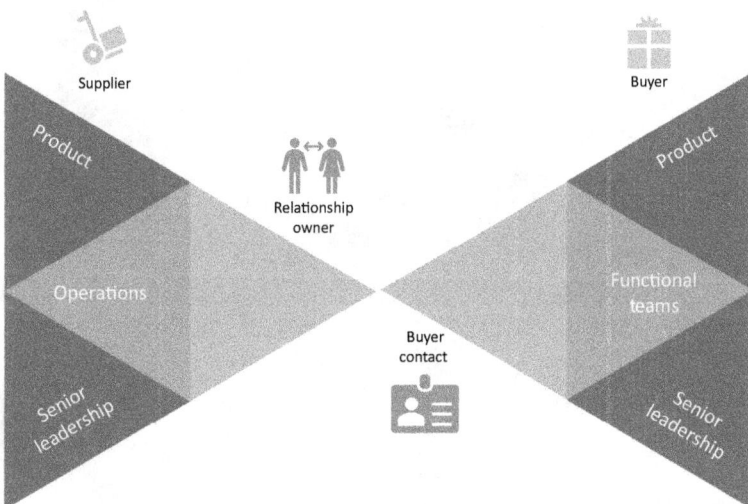

Figure 15.1 Bowties

In the figure above, we can see that your key account is essentially owned and managed by two individuals. Without a concerted and well-documented plan, the danger is that you do not bring to bear all the assets available to your organization in the pursuit of a stickier and more growth-orientated relationship going forward.

The Diamond Approach to Key Account Management

The more sustainable and results-driving alternative to the bowtie model adopts a diamond shape. Here, the individual overseeing overall business relationships on each side can facilitate interaction across the entire diversity of your people organization. This serves to strengthen the overall commitment and alignment of both parties and allows for your strengths on the ground to become more apparent. There is still an overall responsible owner of the account of course, but they help to take the lead to promote wider and deeper engagement using all channels at their disposal to involve more people to forge connections from the C-suite down. This

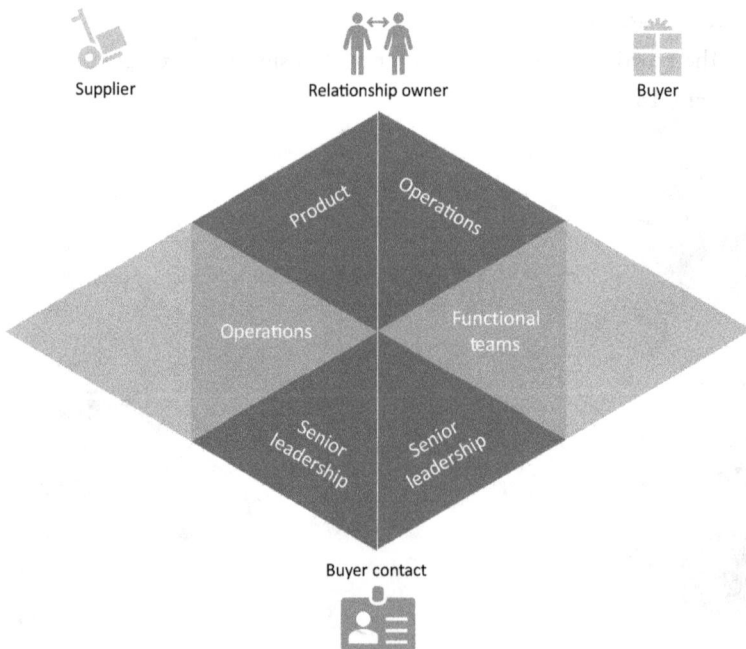

Figure 15.2 Diamonds versus bowties

enables deeper engagement, value, and opportunity to be unlocked. This can be something of a challenge to bring into life at an organization without potentially ruffling some feathers and could come at the cost of losing some people. When considering this move, make sure that the values and behaviors you are seeking culturally are well communicated upfront. The diamond approach is really the epitome of a building bridges to win culture.

In the Figure 15.2, the two partnering organizations are essentially mirrored toward each other. In these scenarios, the account owners now helm a holistic strategy aimed at further maturing and deepening the partnership.

If you are implementing this change, again ensure that you gather your observations and data to help you in proposing changes to existing structures and approaches to key account management. Remember that asking for individual sales plans is a part of this and will lend evidence or inputs to your case. The first step is to explain what the goal is and how your proposed approaches will make a substantive impact. This starts with the implicit risk of owning a whale account and therefore the need to defend as well as expand the relationship. Then, build the case for potential areas for investigation, in terms of expanding your current pot of business.

If you are in an organization where moving to a sales-focused structure around key accounts is needed, bear in mind that training could be a necessary investment. Set appropriate KPIs on the work needed to further develop the account relationships through opening up pipeline opportunity. Follow through and review often.

A good first step is to review the current relationship maps across the client's C-suite. Understand and frame those relationships and be honest about those you do not currently have access to. Ensure that any QBR is delivering insight and is a two-way sharing process, then begin to find ways to add value by opening up the account so that your key people marry off to their counterpoints on the customer side.

The Figure 15.3 shown below, shows a level of connectivity to a global key account. By ensuring a cadence of QBRs and regular check-ins across this network, you can ensure that strategies are created in partnership and that all opportunities within the account are understood, mapped and executed upon.

CEO
Global CFO
Global treasurer
Head of finance
Head of strategy
CFO Americas
CFO EMEA

President
Your CFO
U.K. EVP
VP commercial
Head of product
Head of strategy

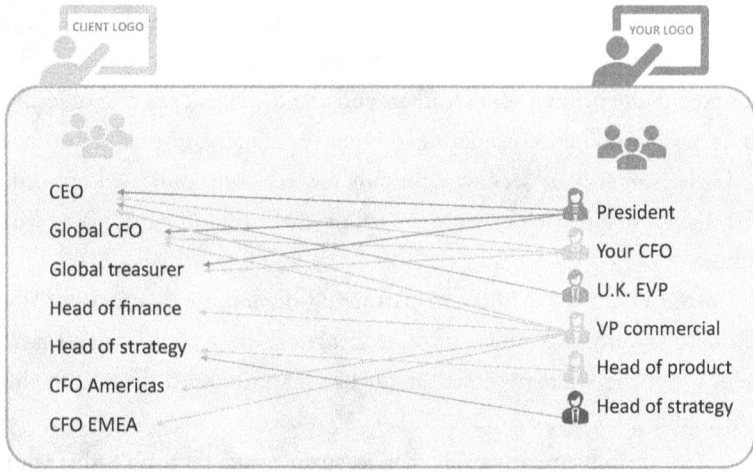

Global acting local—winning it together

Figure 15.3 Account mapping exec to exec

Embedding a Land and Expand Approach

Whether this is a brand new initiative or enhancing current approaches, set your account-facing people a task to map out the status of the current relationship. The client review template in Figure 15.4 is a great way to get this work underway.

Customer "Land and Expand" Template
YOUR LOGO Customer:
Relationship owner:
Executive owner:

Financial results

Relationship overview

Customer description
• Describe
Relationship
• Describe
Commercials
Product
Engagement
Relationship map

2022 highlights
1. Describe
2. Describe
3.

2023 priorities
1. Describe
2. Describe
3.

Os and Rs
Opportunities
• Describe
Risks
• Describe

Figure 15.4 Land and expand

Key Client Review Template

This internal review is about honestly presenting the current key account relationship status across a number of themes. It is designed to surface topics which can be discussed in a deeper dive session where strategies, actions, and investments might be agreed upon.

This exercise should be refreshed annually using a template such as the one shown above. The outputs should then inform the annual sales plan for key accounts.

Financial Results

Always start with the numbers and report these in a relevant way for your business and industry. An analysis of the previous year to this year is also useful here to show velocity.

Relationship Overview

In this section, capture the key dynamics and events currently happening in the account. Report on the strengths and blockers as you see them. Highlight any threats and opportunities in relationship terms as well.

Highlights

List any wins or moments to celebrate in the account. Consider how well the client is acknowledging these and if any could be used in joint marketing initiatives.

Key Initiatives

List here the main focuses and must-win areas for you within this financial year. Try to keep the list succinct and achievable. It is easier to execute fully on one to three focused initiatives; anything more could become distracting and could prevent the completion of any. It is better to add to the list only when goals have been met, than to try and shoot for the stars.

Opportunities and Risks (Os and Rs)

Opportunities and risks. What is on the horizon in terms of areas to develop or concerns we might have in terms of competitive approaches or dynamics in the market? Within this section, it is important to list the dollar values in terms of these opportunities and risks. Make sure that these tie back to your sales plan and, if sufficiently important, to your cornerstone as well.

Defend, Land, and Expand

Specific time-bound initiatives planned for the next period. Impacts should also be captured here. Ensure that the initiatives are captured in high-level terms. The detail can be discussed and actions captured and ascribed outside of this document.

Evolve and Develop

Here, some big bets and/or investments should be noted, with their potential impacts on the bottom-line results. These could include new markets, product enhancements, and other critical initiatives not currently available. Consider here as well what the ask is in terms of investment or prioritization.

What Needs to Be True to Win

List here a summary of the additional help needed to win. This could be executive sponsorship, client events, entertainment, and other critical investment required. Again, the asks and the impacts must be clear and concise.

Takeaways

- *Your existing customer base is potentially a huge area for development.*
- *Ensure relationship management is acting as a part of the sales team.*

- *Undertake client reviews and ensure that feedback is captured and actioned.*
- *Use diamonds as opposed to bowtie structures to fully unlock client potential.*
- *Utilize the existing client review template as part of your sales and budgetary planning.*

CHAPTER 16

Reviews and Pivots

Chapter Summary

- Set up your reporting and cadence to allow you to monitor your progress to plan.
- Weekly pipeline meetings are tactical; monthly and quarterly sales reviews are more strategic, with a deeper dive to understand current velocity as well as what we did right, where we went wrong, and what we can change.

Now you have your plans, you need to consider what are the data points and inputs that will show you whether you are tracking successfully to plan as intended. Every good plan needs to be revisited, and pivots inevitably need to be considered. A vital part of your role is to elevate yourself to track progress, look around corners, think forward and plug gaps, or exploit presented opportunities as they appear.

It is highly unlikely that all of your planned outcomes will come off as originally conceived, especially if you are in complex industries. This is why it is essential to revisit your planning and to think of those plans as living documents. The cornerstone is likely to stay fixed, but the route to the destination may well change or be tweaked.

> *Everyone has a plan until they get punched in the mouth.*
> —Mike Tyson, interview

This is where the routine cadence that you set with your sales teams becomes super important as this will give you the strongest sense of how you are traveling. At this point of the journey, you are likely to be 60 or 90 days in; by now, you will have a true handle on the business and you will have set your vision and built your plans.

The job of creating your behaviors, which are now shaping your culture, will be advanced. You should be seeing signs of the new setting as you observe the team interacting. Your sales plan will be underway; perhaps there is still deeper analysis to do on the customer base and approaches, but, armed with focused use cases as well as the principles of focus and finish and land and expand, your team will be fully engaged anew with the market.

Now, it becomes vital that you can monitor the health of your progress and begin to see around corners to ready yourself and the team, should you need to pivot or reset elements in pursuit of your goal.

Example Cadence—Results, Activities, Support, Training, and Mentoring

When starting out or turning around an environment, I would always seek a cadence of weekly, monthly, and quarterly sales meetings. This would of course run alongside the one-to-ones and daily interactions that there would be across the group, focusing on specific customers or deals in play.

The Figure 16.1 shows the ways you might focus the sales team gatherings. From tactical to strategic, create an agenda that serves your plan in action and helps to share the learnings and voice of the market that you are picking up along the way.

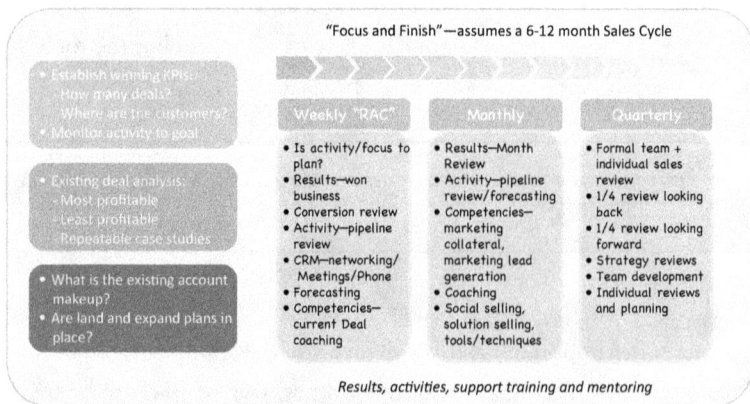

"Focus and Finish"—assumes a 6-12 month Sales Cycle

	Weekly "RAC"	Monthly	Quarterly
• Establish winning KPIs: How many deals? Where are the customers? • Monitor activity to goal	• Is activity/focus to plan? • Results—won business • Conversion review • Activity—pipeline review • CRM—networking/ Meetings/Phone • Forecasting • Competencies— current Deal coaching	• Results—Month Review • Activity—pipeline review/forecasting • Competencies— marketing collateral, marketing lead generation • Coaching • Social selling, solution selling, tools/techniques	• Formal team + individual sales review • 1/4 review looking back • 1/4 review looking forward • Strategy reviews • Team development • Individual reviews and planning
• Existing deal analysis: • Most profitable • Least profitable • Repeatable case studies			
• What is the existing account makeup? • Are land and expand plans in place?			

Results, activities, support training and mentoring

Figure 16.1 *Metrics and monitoring*

The Weekly Meeting

This is a meeting to set the agenda of the week and focus on the most mature deals in the pipeline as well as a moment to think on the support needed to further develop or close these deals. This is a highly tactical check in meeting. Closing off would be a sense of what new conversations or deals were entering the pipeline, with a special focus on identifying critical or complex deals to be developed outside of the group setting.

Running primarily off the CRM, this meeting will give you a sense of the trajectory of your business. You will be able to focus on those mature deals with emphasis on progression and closing. You will also quickly begin to get a sense of how your deal cycles work and where things are potentially getting held up. Pricing reviews and individual client strategy meetings and groups would meet outside of this cadence to support the momentum of deal making.

The Monthly Meeting

A deeper dive into the pipeline and CRM can be undertaken with the team on a monthly basis. Here, I would be focused on the overall health of the pipeline: reviewing results, won and lost business, followed by analysis, solving for any issues pertaining to a lack of refreshment at the top of the funnel or deals getting stuck in the middle or mature stages, and always bringing a focus to deals that could be brought forward as much as possible through focus and finish principles. This is a much deeper and strategic look at developments toward the plan.

An analysis of lost deals and competitive behaviors can also be discussed at this meeting as well as action or suggestions on training or other required support. Case studies of why clients went with us, the approaches undertaken, and competition updates can also work well in the monthly setting, alongside celebration of successes.

The Quarterly Meeting

This would be a vital meeting in the course of prosecuting the year, involving a critical look back and projection forward on the state of the business reaching its set objectives. Within this context, a holistic full business review of finances, highlights, misfires, and areas to improve can also be undertaken. Consider then:

- What did we do right?
- Where did we go wrong?
- What can we change?

This deeper review can be undertaken to ensure that any course correction would be discussed and implemented as a team, with full understanding of the implications of the current speed of travel and focus. This can also be a good time to conduct formal deeper dive one-to-ones across the group. If you are not using quarterly meetings to have one-to-one reviews across the team and leaving these to HR and landmark half-yearly or annual reviews, you are in my opinion creating unnecessary risk in terms of building your momentum juggernaut.

The quarterly meeting is also an excellent time to schedule learning sessions, especially focusing on those topics which are helping the team to raise their game.

Establish Mentoring Programs

As part of your coaching and development of your team, consider if it is possible within your organization to set up a mentoring path. You will have in your team individuals who, with guidance, could improve their go-to market sales skills, or who have the potential for leadership. Ensuring that their potential is realized is not only good for the business but key for ongoing retention and loyalty, as your folks will feel they are seen and invested in.

Speak to your HR business partners about implementing an internal program and think about folks in the organization who could have the skills and experience to help guide and develop these talents. Investing in your key talent in this way is another form of reinforcing your culture build. Feeling that you are personally growing, being identified and developed for your potential or performance as an individual, is a massive motivator, helping to not only cement your teams, but also helping to create the employer of choice reputation in the market as well.

All Good Plans Are Flexible

Good data, cadence, and monitoring help you identify the need to tweak the plan, if required. It is also good to bring the team into the process. Present the challenges and brainstorm with them on ways to find solutions. Involve them directly and bind them to the cause in a creative mindset toward problem solving. By doing this, you will demonstrate that you are all in this together as one team. Top-down messaging is never likely to blossom creativity when it is most needed. At worst, it can produce panic and an impetus to score any deal, no matter whether good for the business or not.

Once decisions have been made collectively, agree on the path, define the expected results, and set timelines for review and delivery of key actions. Ideally, your tweaks and pivots will succeed and allow you to again focus on lifting yourself beyond your current financial year.

Takeaways

- *Ensure that you establish a cadence of review with your team that delivers insights on your progress to plan.*
- *Make sure that these meetings are meaningful and aligned to your goals; make sure your team is getting as much as you are out of the sessions.*
- *Fully involve the team in reviews and if necessary, pivots and tweaks to plan.*
- *Consider mentoring as part of your coaching and development program.*
- *Do not forget your longer term planning and strategy—you are not simply here for the current financial year alone.*

CHAPTER 17

How to Create Culture, Cadence, and Followership

Chapter Summary

- In building your culture, understand your leadership brand through identification of your values and attributes.
- In this chapter, we look at some techniques and processes to help you understand yourself better, so as to enhance your authentic people-first leadership, giving you the best chance of delivering cultural change that sticks.

Building culture is a process. It does not happen overnight; it requires focus, interest, and a desire to maintain and defend it. Culture is fragile; a bad hire, a merger or acquisition, or a change of leadership can all have unforeseen impacts. Within this book, I have attempted to show a layered pathway to creating and maintaining your culture. Do consider your culture build as if it were a layer cake and take time to build each section to last.

Example Culture Cake Ingredients

Spend any time on Instagram or TikTok and, soon enough, you will go down the rabbit hole of the best pastry chefs in the world. (I highly recommend Cedric Grolet.) If you do, not only will you soon be craving pastry delights, but you will also see the meticulous, careful buildup of each sweet layer until the finished article can be decorated and enjoyed. It is entirely the same in your business: miss a layer or a step in your culture build and you will not have the most desired end result. Attend to each

Example culture cake
ingredients

Figure 17.1 The culture cake

layer with passion and care and you will create a performance working culture delight.

The Figure 17.1 above shows potential elements critical to building a performance culture that will inspire and sustain year after year. Consider what layers you need to build. Culture is not simply about having an office where all can gather. Neither is it enjoying banter in the pursuit of your business. If you want to transform your results and inject creativity, passion and velocity within a fun, hard-working group, you must embark on a more holistic approach. Once you have done this, live it, police it and enjoy it, because you have accomplished something rare: a working environment where people will thrive and enjoy their time, where they will remember, always, their growth and achievements.

What Are Your Core Values as a Leader?

Just as the vision of the chef manifests itself in the finished cake, the business or sales leader should also reflect on their vision, passions, and skill sets, as well as the desired outcomes one wants to get to. Whatever the starting point of your journey, you should take a moment to reflect on the attributes you possess, or need to develop, in order to set about building the first layers of your sales team culture. There is a necessary vulnerability to people leadership in a people-first context. This essentially boils down to giving something of yourself, your values, and your principles.

By showing these traits, you will gain more followership, especially when aligned to a well-conceived and focused plan. You will also come across as more authentic to your team. The more progressed you are in your career, it is likely you will have come to know yourself better. You will have worn the scars and victories of management and likely received much conducive feedback along the way. You will have adapted and learnt from those around you, as much as from your direct experiences. It is likely you will have a sense of your core motivations, your values, approaches, and perhaps even a philosophy in terms of your approach to sales leadership. If you are not entirely there or beginning to shape and define these, take time now to think about this as part of your growth journey.

Remember that curiosity and a growth mindset are critical to authentic leadership. The best leaders I have known throughout my career have never considered themselves fully formed. Some of the most wonderful people managers I know maintain regular and often close executive mentoring relationships, for example, no matter how senior or experienced they are. They use these to help them to best strategize for new challenges and even to test how they are turning up and delivering.

An example of this is one of the greatest bosses and people leaders I have known. He brought his executive coach to a full leadership offsite, where we were settling principles of culture and best working practices, as part of planning to kick forward into a particularly ambitious growth program. The coach was introduced to the group and was there to essentially observe our boss and his interactions. This is an incredibly brave and vulnerable action within itself. To see this from one of the most senior and experienced executives, shows that there are always areas to work on; we are after all only humans. Humility and vulnerability are key qualities to develop as people-first leaders.

If you are in the promotion stage or are invited to come and reset an environment, it is worth going through the exercise of reflecting on where you are at as a leader. As we have covered, these are moments when you can feel especially exposed and under a heightened glare of scrutiny from everyone around you. Taking the time to reflect on your strengths, skills, and the journey that has brought you to your present moment can offer a solid foundation for decision making, problem solving, and the facing of new challenges. It can also help ensure that you are setting realistic goals, building on your achievements, and cultivating a positive mindset.

At the beginning of your career, it can be harder to do this of course. There will be a lot of noise and competing attention for your focuses. You must be more conscious of what you represent as opposed to what you do not know. It can seem daunting to undertake what might be considered an introspective exercise, when you probably feel the pressure of action. As such, I would suggest the following techniques to help give you a baseline.

Development of Your Personal Brand

Think of three statements to describe you and your leadership style. These could be, for example:

- *Strategic and goal driven*: Setting clear and measurable goals for the team, developing sales strategies that align with the overall business objectives, and focusing on key performance indicators, while guiding the team to achieve targets through well-versed tactics and plans.
- *Coach and mentor*: Prioritizing the development of team members and the provision of ongoing coaching and feedback to enhance individual and collective performance.
- *Customer obsessed and relationship driven*: Emphasis on the importance of meeting customer needs, leadership demonstrated through the forging of long-term and mutually beneficial relationships that demonstrate customer loyalty, and active listening and encouragement of effective communication with a focus on delivering value to clients.

If you are struggling to come up with appropriate statements, do not write them straight away. Instead and as a part of this exercise, first think of what values and attributes you hold dear and how you manifest these. Think of what these might be and how they got you here to this point of your life and career. For example as follows.

Your Values

1. *Family*: My family comes first. I strive to maintain strong, loving relationships.
2. *Integrity*: I believe in honesty, transparency, and ethical behavior in all aspects of life.
3. *Growth*: I value personal and professional growth, I am curious and look for opportunities to develop, and I seek uncomfortable situations to progress this journey and my learning.
4. *Empathy*: I aim to understand and support others' emotions and perspectives.
5. *Community*: I aim to make positive impacts and to serve my community.
6. *Health*: Physical and mental health is an important driver for me.

Your Attributes

1. *Team player*: I work well together within a team and seek diverse, divergent, and even challenging perspectives and contributions.
2. *Curious*: I am interested in those around me and in new ideas, approaches, and experiences.
3. *Patience*: I approach situations with calmness and understanding, even in testing circumstances.
4. *Coaching mentality*: I do not seek to provide solutions for others, rather I mentor them in helping them find their own solutions for their better and more confident development.
5. *Reliability*: Others can count on me to be consistent and supportive always.
6. *Unbiased*: I spend my time and energies widely and seek all inputs and contributions.
7. *Creative*: I push myself to find creative and innovative approaches.
8. *Resilient*: I react well to change and nebulous situations, seeking the positives and opportunities for growth.

The previous list is not comprehensive so do take time to think of what best describes your make up. Do not shy away from any that you might find or consider to be negative or a current weakness either. Be honest.

Once you have gathered the list of your values and attributes, then you can think about which most hold true to yourself. Again, if you are unsure, ask for critical feedback from others about how you match up to these and how they perceive that you show up. Go to colleagues and family and ask for their candid unvarnished opinions. Asking for feedback is again a highly vulnerable position to put yourself in. Be prepared to be gracious for all the feedback you receive. If the feedback you receive is not so good, then treat all inputs as genuine gifts, especially if you have been blind to the traits described. All feedback and especially that on areas to improve, is to be treasured. Remember leadership, like culture building, is a journey.

If you are considering the role of feedback in personal and professional development, consider the work of Dr. Tasha Eurich. Dr. Tasha is an organizational psychologist and New York Times bestselling author and has written extensively on this topic. In her book *Insight: The Surprising Truth About How Others See Us, How We See Ourselves, and Why the Answers Matter More Than We Think*, Copyright © 2018 by Dr. Tasha; Eurich explores the importance of self-awareness and feedback in achieving success and fulfilment.

Once you have gathered your inputs and some critical feedback, list your values again in the light of what you have learnt and use this to develop two or three sentences as a branding statement of yourself and your leadership style. Make sure you write this down, so you see it every day as part of living your statement authentically.

Me, We, and Work

This is an exercise in showing how critical aspects of your life show up as dimensions of who you are and how they interconnect. This helps again to determine your core values and drivers. It also allows you to set goals and priorities into each area. There is also a clearly cultural aspect to this exercise. Another benefit of this technique is that it can ensure that you set balanced and fulfilling life goals, encompassing "me," "we," and "work."

Me

1. *Personal values*: List the core values, beliefs, and principles that guide your life and matter the most to you.
   a. Examples: integrity, health, growth, and creativity.
2. *Personal goals*: Outline short- and long-term goals, which could be related to well-being, hobbies, and personal and professional development, anything important to you as an individual.
   a. Examples: achieve work–life balance, run a marathon, or learn a musical instrument.

We

1. *Relationships*: Identify the key relationships and connections in your life. This can include family, friends, and other meaningful relationships.
   a. Examples: strengthen the bond with family, nurture relationships, and build a supportive social network.
2. *Community involvement*: Mention community projects, causes, or commitments that are important to you. This could be charitable support, possibly the mentoring you undertake within or externally to your network, volunteering, sports, or coaching.
   a. Examples: support a charity, volunteer time to coach, mentor, and give back to your network.
3. *Team*: Mention what you aspire to see within your professional teams across a number of areas.

Work

1. *Career values*: List the values and principles that guide your professional life. What matters most in work-related decisions?
   a. Examples: innovation, leadership, and work–life balance.
2. *Professional goals*: Specify your career goals and aspirations. Think both short and long term.
   a. Example: promotion or achievement of defined milestones.

3. *Skills development:* Mention the skills you want to acquire or develop, improve, or learn.
   a. Example: enhanced leadership skills, improved public speaking, and developing mentoring skills.
4. *Work–life Integration:* Highlight how you aim to balance professional and personal to achieve overall well-being.
   a. Example: establish boundaries.

A Letter to My Future Self

Now you have considered what has got you here and what your current makeup is, consider where you want to be. Writing a letter to your future self can be a meaningful and reflective exercise. It allows you to set goals, express your current thoughts and feelings, and provide yourself with a glimpse into your past and your journey when you eventually open it.

1. *Choose a future date:* As with all exercises, making it time bound is part of the commitment. It could be a year, three years, or longer. Make sure this is a meaningful timeframe for you.
2. *Reflect on your current leadership state:* What are the key events and experiences happening right now? Reflect on your achievements, challenges, and personal growth to this point. This is about what you hope to be, or to achieve, or how people will see you showing up in your role.
3. *Set your intentions:* What will you hope to have accomplished by the time you open the letter? Outline your aspirations, personal and professional. Include specific goals as well as broader themes and values.
4. *Write your letter:* Start with a friendly greeting and encouraging tone. Address yourself as if a close friend. Share your thoughts and your feelings and be honest, vulnerable, and open. Discuss hopes and dreams as well as future expectations. Express gratitude and be thankful for the experiences that have helped shape you.
5. *Keep it personal:* You are writing this for yourself and your journey; make it yours.
6. *Seal and store the letter:* Store the letter "to my future self" and remind yourself to review this when the time comes.

7. *Open and reflect*: Take the time to reflect on your past and on your thoughts and intentions. Compare this state to your current one and see how you have grown and changed. Be kind to yourself and reward your bravery.

Focusing on Yourself as Part of Your Culture Build

These exercises are all about focusing on you as a critical element of your culture build through the lens of passion and the focus of being the leader. It is important you recognize in yourself the qualities that will help you create your culture and emphasize these. Acknowledge your weaknesses as well; perhaps you are an introvert, many of us in sales are. Identify these areas, acknowledge them, and work on them.

It is too easy to know aspects of yourself without ever really isolating them, unpacking them fully, and analyzing why they may or may not be holding you back. These exercises ensure that you are taking responsibility for your growth and journey as you shape the culture that will be an ongoing winning and sustainable proposition.

Takeaways

- *Check on how unkind you are being to yourself.*
- *Use the exercises to reflect on the stories you are telling yourself.*
- *Consider what mental rewiring and active steps you may need to take to retrain your thinking and approaches in certain circumstances.*
- *If you are building the best culture cake, you are a fundamental ingredient and the better you know yourself, your drivers, and how you actually represent these, the better you will be at creating followership and culture within your teams.*
- *Remember also that the previous lists are dynamic and will evolve over time as your priorities and your circumstances change. You will grow as a leader.*

(Continued)

(*Continued*)

- *Remember you are on a learning journey and your culture will also evolve and change—sometimes for the better, sometimes for the worst—but that you hold a responsibility to yourself and your team. Remaining curious and open to learning is a part of helping to drive your own self-growth as well as that of the team around you.*

CHAPTER 18

Feedback and Availability

Chapter Summary

- Part of building a culture, and being an authentic leader, is to be available to provide feedback and support as required.
- Consider the environments in which you work and whether these support your authentic culture.

Product, people, and passion—when you have this combination, you are likely winning. That said, the greatest rule in business or life for that matter, is to never be complacent. Enjoy the successes of course and celebrate the wins and the recognition of the culture and environment you have built with your people, but remain vigilant.

The day-to-day life in a well-operating sales environment is one of collaboration, problem solving, monitoring pipeline, tracking specific deal progress, pricing, strategizing, engaging with key clients, planning events and whatever formatted company happenings you have lined up throughout the year. It is also about being adept at creatively addressing individual tactical issues and navigating crises as and when they occur. Whether it is adapting strategies, offering innovative solutions, or providing hands-on support during tough moments, the leader ensures the team is well equipped to handle various situations to continue achieving their sales objectives. Of course, there will be the continued mentoring and coaching of your team to focus on as well.

In order to maintain and reinforce your culture and to be an effective coach or mentor, it is important that expectations are clear and inherent in the culture you have developed. It is also important that you are available and open to feedback. Consider then that:

- You are available to anyone in the team, anytime, on any channel.
- Your availability is not limited to a few, that favoritism is not a perception or a factor.
- Prior to escalation, the team would have taken appropriate steps and measures to explore options and outcomes.
- You trust your people to bring to you topics that are affecting them or their customers directly and openly.
- No issue or idea is a bad one to surface and discuss.
- Good ideas can come from anywhere and should be encouraged.
- You will provide support and perhaps aircover to allow your people to act with freedom and expression and to be their real selves, bound to the mission of winning for your customers.
- You will not simply be prosecuting the current financial year and its goals but looking forward to where you and the business will be in three- to five-years' time.

The greatest leaders I have known always take the opportunity to ask for input constantly and ask how they can help you in practically every interaction. They also make themselves available and show an interest in their people beyond the day-to-day challenges of work. A large part of this is self-awareness, which also involves the gathering of objective feedback from colleagues and employees.

Authentic engagement is a huge part of building culture and making work a fun environment to be in. I would encourage this to be face-to-face as much as possible and do beware of the electronic channels. E-mail, WhatsApp, text, Slack, Teams, Skype, Webex, Facebook (Meta), and countless other channels inundate our working lives these days. Nothing beats face-to-face engagement.

This is especially so since the pandemic, when these tools became ever more vital for communication and engagement. They cannot and should not ever be used as a replacement for time spent together, as you will never make the true connection that you can face-to-face. Be conscious of this and make sure that you have the blend of remote and in-person interaction right to support and enable the growth, development, and maintenance of your culture.

Takeaways

- *Be authentically available to your teams,*
- *Beware of electronic channels of communication and ensure you have your in-person and remote balance optimized for your team's benefit.*

Conclusion

Fun

In the ever-evolving landscape of business and management, one principle has emerged as an unwavering beacon of success: people-first leadership. This philosophy, rooted in the profound understanding that the heart of any organization is its people, has transformed the way we approach leadership and organizational culture.

Throughout this book, we have explored the profound impact of putting people first within the context of sales leadership. True people-first leaders prioritize the well-being, growth, and happiness of their teams above all else. They recognize that exceptional results stem from engaged, motivated, and empowered individuals who feel valued, heard, and supported.

But becoming a people-first leader is not a destination; it's a continuous journey of growth and self-discovery. It's about learning to be the best cultural leader you can be, day by day.

- *Authenticity and vulnerability are key*: People-first leadership starts with authenticity. It's about being genuine, transparent, and true to yourself. Authentic leaders inspire trust and create an environment where others feel safe to be themselves.
- *Empathy fuels trust*: Empathy is the cornerstone of effective leadership. Understanding the perspectives, needs, and emotions of your team members fosters a deeper connection. It's about genuinely caring for the people you lead.
- *Growth mindset*: The path to becoming a better cultural leader is marked by a growth mindset. Embrace challenges, learn from failures, and constantly seek opportunities to improve, both as a leader and as a person. Invest also in your own growth and development through reading, mentorship, coaching, and feedback.

- *Communication is key*: Effective communication is the lifeblood of a people-first leader. Listen actively, communicate clearly, and foster open, honest, and constructive dialogues within your team and across your organization. Building bridges to win starts with every facet of the organization understanding and aligning to what you are trying to achieve in sales.
- *Lead by example*: Cultural leadership is not just about what you say; it's about what you do. Be the embodiment of the values and behaviors you want to instill within your organization.
- *Adaptability and inclusivity*: The world is ever changing. As a people-first leader, you will need to be adaptable, embracing diversity, equality, and inclusion as core principles in your leadership style to create a culture where everyone can thrive. Celebrate this diversity and encourage it in the ideas that can help shape your business.

It is also a unique journey. Take the time to define your values and mission. Discover your own style and refine it over time. In conclusion, people-first leadership is a powerful force that has the potential to elevate individuals and organizations to new heights. People are at the very heart of every successful sales endeavor.

And Finally… Fun

A word about fun. Sales and sales leadership should be fun. Sales is one of the ultimate people businesses and if you love people and interacting with a diverse group set upon solving challenges, then sales can be the most rich and rewarding career there is.

I, for one, have been blessed by the people I have met, the growth and experiences I have absorbed, and the opportunity for travel and working across multiple countries and cultures.

Sometimes, however, you will find yourself in sales environments that are not fun. It is evident to say that if sales and being part of a sales organization is not fun, then something is likely to be out of kilter and you need to diagnose what that is as a priority.

Typically, pressure can be one of the main reasons for a sales environment to be emotion and energy draining. Pressure in this context could be the result of slipping momentum toward targets or a strategy that is not working. It could also be a symptom of a product that is not addressing the needs of the market and a disconnect between the leadership, commercial, and product elements of the company.

If there is lack of clarity on where to play and how to win, this can badly affect the morale. If pressure is also applied, then you may find that your folks are as focused on finding new opportunities elsewhere as they are on new sales. Pressure can turn easily into firefighting, which again is not fun, but speaks to a lack of information in terms of what needs to be true to reverse the trend.

What I have tried to lay out in the previous chapters, is a pathway to quickly becoming expert in your business, and routes to identify the key growth engines to allow you to get beyond the pure focus in your current financial year, and the challenges you are confronting and solving for within it. The pathway to achieving this most effectively is through your people and culture.

You will have to pivot, and you will have to adapt: these things are inevitable. You will never eliminate these tactical and strategic challenges of course, nor would you want to; after all, each deal has its own dynamics that you need to be in control of before the signed order comes in. Get the people element right and the core components will look after themselves, as will your results.

The real fun is when you see the fruits of your labors in cultural terms: when you witness your team working in unison, finding their own solutions, and bringing the customers on the journey with them. Then you know your engine is running smoothly; you can look forward to the next destinations and build your plans in terms of where the company can be in the longer term. Instead of being the mechanic, you can focus on adding the oil and the fuel to get you to where you are going faster.

There are many pleasures in a life of sales. I always used to savor the sweet moment when a client was talking among their team about my solution in their language and putting their people's names to buying actions. This was a moment of pure magic; you knew you could simply shut up and listen and, if asked a question, reflect the answer to them in reinforcement of their language and processes. It was the ultimate buying signal.

In the context of sales leadership, there are similarly magical moments to equally savor: when you can sit and listen to the hum of your office and your team in action. This is the moment you know your work in building a culture has paid off.

There is focus and professionalism, mixed in with good humor. There is an openness to new ideas and approaches, escalations are minimized, and cross-functional collaboration focused on the customer and improvements abound. You are celebrating together and learning through review about mistakes. Diversity and honesty are respected and enjoyed and difficult conversations can be had in a safe psychological space.

It's a unique buzz when the team is ambitious, happy, settled, supporting one another, and having fun—when being at work is a pleasure. It is not just about the sales team either. The supporting functions are involved and part of the journey; you can see the collaboration across all the customer-owning teams. Account plans are being formalized with all stakeholders; there is palpably *one* team thinking and action across the board.

Enjoy this for a moment, reflect on the journey, and bask in the strong energy and infectious hum around your colleagues. It is a pleasure to be among this smooth running engine, you can feel good that the plan is being executed and that the engine is propelling you successfully toward your goal. But also continue to invest in this culture, be jealous about it, and watch for anything that might damage it, as you can be sure your culture is a living, breathing thing that can easily decline or shatter if taken for granted.

Do though take a moment to understand how you have arrived here. This will be in large part because you:

- Simplified your business and cultural goals into your cornerstone one pager.
- Gained buy-in by communicating and aligning the top-level goals with the team and all stakeholders across the business.

- Reinforced buy-in and belief by creating the bottom-up sales plan.
- Focused down on key must-win elements—focus and finish.
- Developed the low-hanging fruit through existing customer plans—land and expand.
- Created a safe and collaborative environment where feedback is shared, and all have a stake in the journey—winning it together.
- Helped your team find their network and their solutions, thereby minimizing escalations.
- Celebrated successes and had fun along the way.

Great leaders convey equal importance on each team member as no one can be a great leader unless they care about their people.

Enjoy the journey and happy selling!

And remember the key message in Figure C.1 as you set about your transformational culture building mission:

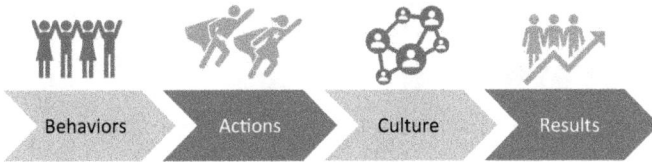

| Behaviors | Actions | Culture | Results |

Figure C.1 Fun—behaviors form culture leading to results

About the Author

Richard Cogswell is a people-first sales leader. He is an organizational team builder who believes that people, vision, values, and behaviors build winning sales cultures. Richard has held multiple senior sales leadership positions within a number of industries, working across EMEA, the United States, and APAC, within startups and listed multinational companies.

Whether newly hired or promoted, or for those with experience already gained on the journey, Richard aims to show a methodology focused on how you might best lay down the foundations for exponential and sustained growth through the sales leadership function, and critically through the catalyst of culture.

You can find out more from Richard at www.richardcogswell.com.

Index

www.ingramcontent.com/pod-product-compliance
Lightning Source LLC
Chambersburg PA
CBHW061155220326
41599CB00025B/4494